INTRODUCTION

Welcome to *Hodder English Gold*. This course book and its two companions represent a quality English curriculum for pupils working at levels 2–4 in Key Stage 3 (S1–3). It has been planned and written to meet the demands of the National Curriculum (and Scottish 5–14 Guidelines) and to maintain a challenging, vigorous and progressive ethos in the classroom. Book 1 introduces pupils to a wide and challenging variety of English experiences and assignments which are then progressively built on and broadened in *Hodder English Gold 2* and *3*. However, teachers may wish to use these books to supplement their own schemes of work, or other materials.

RAISING STANDARDS AND COVERING NATIONAL CURRICULUM REQUIREMENTS

We have taken as our prime directive the advancement of pupil learning. All the materials in *Hodder English Gold* have been trialled in the classroom by English teachers to offer the very best of current practice. Units have been developed to cover the National Curriculum in England, Wales and Northern Ireland and the 5–14 Guidelines in Scotland. At the same time, we know that pupils in the early levels of literacy need explicit instruction and scaffolded activities. We have provided both in the context of purposeful work and quality texts. Each book contains one unit of work which addresses basic skills as a focus of work in its own right and consolidation activities have been built in later.

Hodder English Gold addresses the appropriate number of set texts and includes many more. Pre-twentieth century literature is amply represented in both fiction and non-fiction. You will find here a catholic range of genres, tones and forms, but we have resisted simplified versions in favour of abridgement. We have made particular efforts to ensure that speaking and listening is fully represented in the series, not merely as incidental group talk but as a purposeful activity in its own right.

STRUCTURE

Hodder English Gold consists of three books, one for each year at Key Stage 3 (years S1–3 in Scotland) and a cassette. Each book is divided into six units, and each of these units represents a half-term's work. The units have been arranged across the three years to establish, revisit and consolidate key skills.

Although the units have been placed in an order which offers pupils a varied and progressive experience of English (for example, the 'Poetry Alive' unit in *Hodder English Gold 1* introduces key skills in poetry which are then picked up in later units), you can use the book in a flexible way, linking units with others or with texts you want to teach.

Whilst we have introduced basic skills directly through key units, and again in the context of others, we also assume that teachers will continue to support individual pupils by giving them feedback on their oral and written performance, and that spelling, punctuation and grammar will be part of this continuing work.

PROGRESSION

Hodder English Gold 1, 2, and *3* form an incremental programme of work with clear goals written with the expressed intention of raising standards in English. The course offers far more than a sequence of self-contained lessons or starting points because progression is built into each unit, between each book and across the course as a whole. Key elements of English are focused on once in each year, and incidentally as a part of other units.

ASSESSMENT

Assessment is an integral part of each unit. However, checklists, recording sheets and assessment grids are deliberately not included, as it is most likely that you have already developed a workable system. Teaching by units enables you to collect evidence of pupils' achievements periodically, and systematically, at the end of each unit. The book provides the pupils with focused tasks and explicit criteria for evaluating how well they are doing, and what they need to improve on. Each unit begins with a clear set of teaching aims and objectives, which will need to be talked through with pupils and revisited as the unit progresses. You will be able to plan the precise nature of your assessments against these aims and objectives. Pupils' own self-assessment is also vital: each unit ends with a page for review and self-assessment or extension tasks.

ACTIVITIES

The initial material and activities of each unit are designed to introduce pupils to the focus for the sequence of work, and to engage their interest. There is then a series of tasks designed to help pupils to develop specific areas of knowledge, understanding and skill. Several pages are given to consolidating new knowledge or skills in context.

USING HODDER ENGLISH GOLD

Many of the units are free-standing and teachers will find them sufficiently flexible to introduce extra material or to extend their use beyond a half-term. Texts have been chosen for their quality and for their richness in classroom study, as well as for their accessibility, and relevance for the age group. Where it has been impractical to reproduce whole texts, we have produced extracts to support the close study of key passages.

In addition, the cassette provides support where it is most helpful. To promote reading skills, we recommend that pupils conduct close study activities using the text as well as the tape so that they can learn how to find particular words, phrases and information in the text. Where icon **A** appears (see below), either on its own or as icon **B** (see below), the text which is being studied is provided on the cassette as well.

For your convenience, a number of pages have been designed as *photocopiable*. These pages contain activities which pupils will do best if they are involved in hands-on work.

A    **B**

HODDER
English
Gold

3

Sue Hackman

Alan Howe

Hodder & Stoughton
A MEMBER OF THE HODDER HEADLINE GROUP

ACKNOWLEDGEMENTS

The publishers would like to thank the following contributors:

John Rowley and David Watkinson	- Unit One, *Horror*
	Unit Two, *Newsroom*
	Unit Five, *Scandal*
Karen Blake and Lynette Newman	- Unit Three, *Macbeth*
Darren Phillips	- Unit Four, *The Language Detective*
Paul Siebert and Adrian Jones	- Unit Six, *Stone Cold*

Copyright Text:
pp110 and 111 from *The Fenland Chronicle* © Sybil Marshall, Penguin; pp138, 139, 142, 146, 154, 155 from *Stone Cold* © Robert Swindells, Penguin; p147 from the BBC TV 'Scene' adaptation of *Stone Cold* © BBC Worldwide Ltd.

Copyright Photographs:
p28 © BFI Stills, Posters and Designs; p38 all photographs © Hodder & Stoughton; p40 [clockwise from top] © Tony Stone, © JT Turner/Telegraph Colour Library, © Ed Horn/Telegraph Colour Library, © N Battersby; p42 © Hodder & Stoughton; p76 © Donald Cooper/Photostage; p78 © Donald Cooper/Photostage; p79 © Donald Cooper/Photostage; p80 © Donald Cooper/Photostage; p140 [top, left] © Peter Dunkley/Life File, [middle] © Andrew Ward/Life File, [right] © Jeremy Hoare/Life File, [bottom, left] © Alan Smith/Tony Stone, [middle] © Andrew Ward/Life File, [right] © David Kampfner/Colorific!, [bottom] © Photo Press; pp147, 148, 149, 152 © Luke Finn/BBC Education by kind permission of the producer Andy Rowley, for 'Scene'; p159 [top] © Photo Press, [bottom] © Photo Press.

Order queries: please contact Bookpoint Ltd, 39 Milton Park, Abingdon, Oxon OX14 4TD.
Telephone: (44) 01235 400414, Fax (44) 01235 400454. Lines are open from 9.00 - 6.00, Monday to Saturday, with a 24 hour message answering service. Email address: orders@bookpoint.co.uk

British Library Cataloguing in Publication Data
A catalogue record for this title is available from The British Library

ISBN 0 340 70183 8

First published 1998
Impression number 10 9 8 7 6 5 4 3 2 1
Year   2002   2001   2000   1999   1998

Copyright © 1998 Sue Hackman and Alan Howe

Designed and typeset by Mind's Eye Design, Lewes.

Printed in Great Britain for Hodder & Stoughton Educational, a division of Hodder Headline Plc, 338 Euston Road, London NW1 3BH by Scotprint Ltd, Musselburgh, Scotland.

CONTENTS

GUIDELINES FOR TEACHERS

HORROR

The unit follows the structure of a typical horror story, moving from openings, settings and suspense to monsters, showdowns and endings.

Teaching points:
Students will bring to this unit a vast knowledge of the horror genre from film, television, anecdote and fiction. It is deep in today's culture and you can draw on it to furnish examples and fuel oral work. You can easily move from this unit to popular fiction, ghost stories, thrillers, the Gothic and wider reading. A collection of related fiction in the classroom, and reading time, will allow students to find parallels in their own reading as they study.

NEWSROOM

The first part of this unit teaches students about the way news is shaped, and how reports apply news values to the available information. The second part is a desk simulation in which pupils assume the role of reporter and make oral bulletins as events develop.

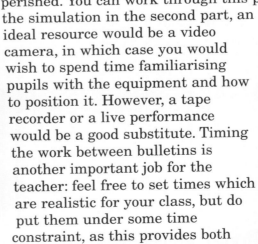

Teaching points:
The first part of the unit is loosely organised around an unfolding story about a warehouse fire in which a pop group may have perished. You can work through this part in a conventional way. For the simulation in the second part, an ideal resource would be a video camera, in which case you would wish to spend time familiarising pupils with the equipment and how to position it. However, a tape recorder or a live performance would be a good substitute. Timing the work between bulletins is another important job for the teacher: feel free to set times which are realistic for your class, but do put them under some time constraint, as this provides both

energy for and insight into the production process. Naturally, current news is a first-class resource, especially if the week's events have a special relevance to your students.

MACBETH

This unit guides pupils through a reading and interpretation of one of the new Key Stage 3 Shakespeare plays. *Macbeth* is likely to be the most popular Key Stage 3 Shakespeare play, and although it has traditionally been taught at Key Stage 4, its exciting plot and relevant themes will make it accessible to younger pupils. Each act is summarised using a cartoon version and pupils are given focused activities that will help them to understand character, motive and action. The play is treated as a script to be brought to life through role-play and active reading strategies.

Teaching points:
You will need a class set of *Macbeth* so that pupils can refer to the script and have access to key scenes. Pupils' appreciation of the play will be enhanced by watching a performance, and we recommend that you support your teaching of the play with extracts from a video production and also make use of the 'Animated' version. Use video selectively to introduce a scene, or interspersed with activities. A number of activities will require some limited drama work and, although you will be able to do this in a conventional classroom, the work will benefit from the flexibility of space offered by a drama studio.

THE LANGUAGE DETECTIVE

This is a unit about Standard English and the way we adapt language in speech and writing to suit the purpose and context.

Teaching points:
Students will have plenty to offer a discussion of the different accents and dialects and an adventurous teacher might build further role-play into this unit. Television also offers a range of language which is easy to capture.
Beware suggesting that non-standard accents and dialects are wrong. The spirit of this unit is to interest students in language itself and then widen their repertoire of voices on and off paper.

Although this unit is largely about the writing process, it offers particularly good opportunities for reading about topical issues in the news and discussion of controversial subject matter.

Teaching points:

The activities focus on the ethics of publication and, later, on the genuine complexity which sometimes face ordinary people as well as reporters. You should build in time for such discussions which arise around these issues. Oral presentation, tape recorders and wall displays are a useful way of providing real audiences for completed work which presents a point of view.

STONE COLD

This award-winning novel by Robert Swindells explores the experience of homelessness in a fictional story that becomes increasingly mysterious and ultimately horrific. A particular feature of the novel is the use of dual narrators: Link, the central character who ends up homeless in London, and Shelter, who appears to help the homeless – or does he? The book was chosen for inclusion in Hodder English Gold as it will provide Year 9 pupils with an accessible book which is also challenging both in its narrative devices and in its content.

Teaching points:

You will need a set of *Stone Cold* to enable you to bridge the key passages that are the main elements of the unit. We suggest that you read most of the novel aloud, encouraging pupils to tackle the reading demands of the passages included in the unit. The unit offers a guided reading of the novel, with carefully structured activities designed to deepen pupils' response and understanding as they go along. Pupils are encouraged to keep a 'Reading Log' as they progress through the novel, as a way of catching their ideas and learning to develop their written response to key moments. Some may need extra support as they begin to write in the way required. Although not essential, your teaching of the unit will be enhanced if you can get hold of the BBC TV 'Scene' adaptation of the novel, both as a way of offering pupils an alternative version of the story to discuss, and to support some of the activities.

Horror

Horror stories are told in both books and films. In this unit you will look at the different parts of a horror story:

- beginnings
- building up tension
- cliffhanger chapter endings
- monsters
- horror settings
- endings

You will develop your skills as:

SPEAKERS AND LISTENERS

by discussing what makes a good horror story

by sharing some of your experiences of horror stories with others

READERS

by reading some examples of horror writing

by looking at different parts of a horror story

WRITERS

by creating a file of your own openings, cliffhanger chapter
   endings and other writing

by writing a successful horror story of your own

Now turn the page and start to write … horribly!

HOW HORRIBLE!

What images do you associate with horror? Think of films, posters, books…

* Make a horror file to keep your work in. Use your horror
images to make a creepy cover.

BEGINNINGS

Look at these opening scenes from an episode of *The X Files*.

- Imagine that you are Randall. Note down all the mysteries you do not understand. Set your work out like this:

① Why operate on John Barnett in the middle of the night?

②

Discuss the following questions in groups:

- Why do film makers like to start a horror film with a mystery?

- How long do you have to wait for the answers to the mysteries – until the middle of the story, or the end?

- Why do you think you are made to wait for mysteries to be solved?

- Can you think of other horror films or books that have beginnings as mysterious as this?

A PLACE OF HORROR

Look at these settings for horror stories.

- In what ways are the settings similar?
- How are they different?

A vast ruined castle, from whose tall black windows came no ray of light, and whose broken battlements showed a jagged line against the moonlit sky…

(From *Dracula* by Bram Stoker)

	Graveyard	City	Mountains	Dust & Cobwebs	Swamp	Castle
Dracula	✔	✘	✔	✔	✘	✔
Beauty and the Beast						
Frankenstein						
Alien						

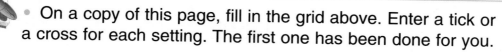

- On a copy of this page, fill in the grid above. Enter a tick or a cross for each setting. The first one has been done for you.

- Make a list of 10 words you could use to describe a dark and horrible place. The first two have been done for you.

> 1 *dark*
> 2 *dreary*
> 3
> 4

- Use these words to describe your own setting for a horror story.

HORROR TRAIN

Now it's your chance to write a mystery opening to a horror
story called 'Horror Train'.

 Look at the cartoon. Now take up the story. Keep the mystery going!

- Think about what the kids feel as the train comes closer.

- Why does it get colder as the train approaches?

- What happens when the train stops?

- Are there any passengers? If so, what do they look like?

- Do the kids get on the train?

- You might use these starters to help you with the first few sentences, or you can make up your own.
  As the train came closer, the kids felt…
  As the train neared the platform, they could see…
  Something was strange about the passengers. They all looked…
  There was a smell of…
  The worst thing of all was the…
  As the doors opened…

CREATE YOUR OWN MONSTER

When a crime has been committed the police make a 'photofit' of the criminal. They do this by fitting together photos of eyes, mouth and other features.

- Create your own photofit monster by fitting together features from the monsters on these pages.
- Invent a name for your monster.

Fachan was an Irish monster with one leg and one eye. Its only hand stuck out of its chest. It chased travellers and jumped on them from behind.

A **banshee** was a wailing woman with fiery red eyes, webbed feet and long streaming hair. She had one nostril and a front tooth that stuck out. A banshee would sit crying on the banks of a river, washing the clothes of a person who was about to die.

Jenny Greenteeth was an evil creature who lived underwater. She drowned anyone who went near the green scum on the surface of the water. This green scum was the only clue to where she was. It was all that anyone ever saw…

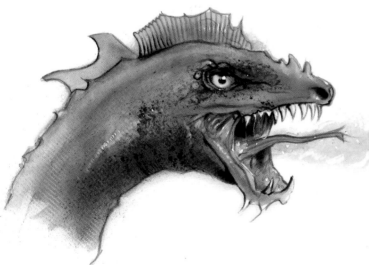

A **basilisk** was a serpent. It was so deadly that if a man put a spear through its body, the poison would spread up the spear and kill the man and his horse. A basilisk could kill by its look or its breath. But it could be killed by its own reflection, or by the crowing of a cockerel.

- Make up a monster of your own. Draw your monster.
- Underneath your drawing write a description of the monster:

1 Describe what your monster can do to people.

2 Explain how it can be killed.

HANGING ON

Horror stories must be exciting, to make us want to read on.
Writers of horror stories often use cliffhanger endings to
build up excitement at the end of a chapter. Look at how the
author builds up the tension in the extract below.

LOST IN THE WOODS

Susan Cooper has just moved to a new house, deep in the
woods. She gets up early to explore without her older brother
Mickey, but gets lost…

I returned to the path again. But with my first step, I heard leaves rustling behind me. I didn't turn round. I quickened my pace.

And I heard it again.

Twigs snapping. Leaves rustling.

My throat suddenly felt dry. Don't panic. Don't panic. 'Who – who's there?' I croaked.

No answer.

I turned back.

Whoa! Which way had I been walking? My head began to spin. I suddenly felt dizzy.

Too dizzy to remember where I had been.

Snap. Snap. Crack. Crunch.

'Who is there?' I called out again. My voice didn't sound all that steady for Super Cooper.

'Mickey, is that you? This isn't funny! Mickey?'

Then I felt something horrible scrape my cheek. Something cold. And sharp.

I couldn't help it. I started to scream.

From *The Barking Ghost* by R. L. Stine

- What do you think is the 'something horrible' that is scraping Susan's cheek? What is going on?

- Discuss what you think is going to happen in the next chapter.
- Now read what actually did happen in the next chapter.

A leaf. A dumb leaf.

Come on Cooper! Get a grip!

Did you get it right? Even if you didn't, you kept on reading – and that is what the writer wanted you to do.

Cliffhanger endings make us want to read on – just like a chapter that ends with the hero hanging from a cliff!

DEAD MAN'S BAY

Now try writing a cliffhanger of your own, starting with the story below.

Jenny has gone on holiday to Dead Man's Bay. Her parents have forbidden her to swim in the bay because sharks have been seen there in the past. But Jenny thinks her parents are making a fuss as usual. She gets up early and goes to Dead Man's Bay for a secret swim…

The story begins like this:

Dead Man's Bay was exactly as Jenny had hoped. A perfect stretch of empty yellow beach. A beautiful, blue sea.
  And not a shark fin in sight.
  Wait until she got back and told her parents she had been swimming in Dead Man's Bay, and nothing had happened! Quickly, she stripped to her swimming costume. Then she sprinted towards the sparkling white surf and dived in.
  At first, it was…

- First finish the chapter. Take the story up to a really frightening point – and stop.

- Write the first few lines of the **next** chapter. Here you can show that Jenny wasn't really in danger after all.

- Swap cliffhangers with a partner. Do **not** pass over your next chapter.

- Try to guess each other's cliffhanger.

- Now swap and see if you were right.

BUILDING UP TENSION

Look at these two versions of a scene:

VERSION A

When Michael reached David's house it was dark. He went in and looked around for a bit. He found David dead in the bath. David had been killed by an escaped murderer, who was still hiding in the loft.

VERSION B

When Michael arrived at his friend's house it was pitch black. To his surprise the front door was ajar. He pushed gently and the door swung inwards.

'David…?' he called softly.

There was no answer.

There was a noise from the sitting room. Michael peered in, but there was only the television.

'Here is the six o'clock news,' said the announcer. 'A dangerous murderer has escaped from a local prison –'

Michael switched it off. Who cared about boring old news?

Suddenly he felt something cold on his nose. He put up his hand and it came away wet. Quickly he went to the stairs, and climbed to the landing. The sound of running water came from the bathroom.

'David, why on earth are you…?'

But his words froze on his lips at the sight of a claw-like hand gripping the edge of the bath.

And blood running down the side…

'David!' he cried.

Through a crack in the ceiling a cruel eye watched Michael rush to his friend.

- Which version builds up the tension best?
- How is the tension built up?
- Which version do you prefer?
- What do you like reading about in that version?

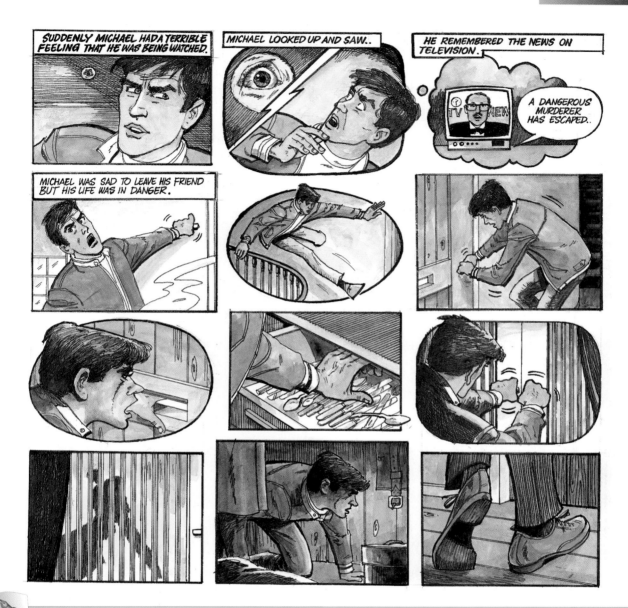

Now continue the story as Michael tries to escape from the house.

- Start when Michael looks up and sees the murderer's eye through a hole in the bathroom ceiling.

- Use any of the ideas suggested above to build up tension, as Michael struggles to escape.

- You can use these starters to help you write the first few sentences, or you can make up your own.

Suddenly Michael had a terrible feeling that he was being…
It was an eye…
At that moment he remembered the news on the television. Immediately he knew…
He did not want to leave his friend David in the bath, but…

- The ending is up to you. It could be a cliffhanger ending.

DRACULA LIVES!

Dracula is the most famous monster. Dracula has a human body but can change into a bat. He has long teeth that he sinks into the necks of his victims to drink their blood. But on the surface he is still a normal man, except for one or two details...

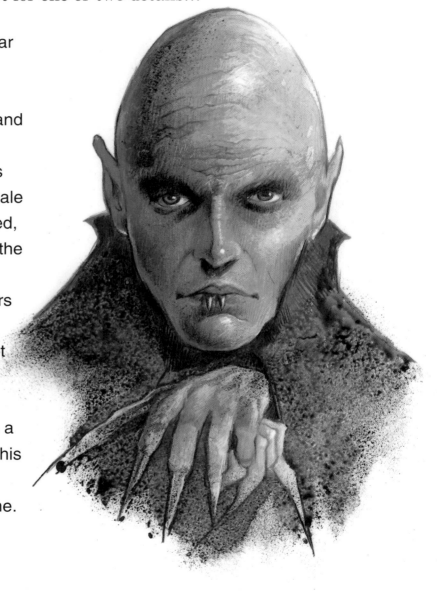

It was a strong face, with peculiar arched nostrils and high domed forehead. His eyebrows were massive. The mouth was fixed and rather cruel looking, with sharp white teeth, which hung over his lip. For the rest, his ears were pale and at the tops extremely pointed, the chin was broad and strong, the cheeks firm though thin.

Strange to say, there were hairs in the centre of his palms. The nails were long and fine, and cut to a sharp point. As the Count leaned over me and his hands touched me, I could not repress a shudder. It may have been that his breath was rank, but a horrible feeling of sickness came over me. I heard from down below in the valley, the howling of many wolves. The Count's eyes gleamed and he said: 'Listen to them – the children of the night. What music they make!'

From *Dracula* by Bram Stoker

- Write down the five most frightening details from this description of Dracula.

Perhaps you have seen other Draculas in films, or in books or comics. Often Dracula seems a normal person on the surface. But one or two little details give him away.

- Imagine that you suspect a new teacher might be Dracula.

- Note down two or three details that suggest that the new teacher might be a vampire.

- Now write your own description of 'The Vampire Teacher'. You may find some words from Bram Stoker's passage to help you.

HORRIBLE HORROR

With his left hand he held both Mrs Harker's hands, his right hand gripped her by the back of the neck, forcing her face down on his bosom. Her white night-dress was smeared with blood, and a thin stream trickled down the man's bare breast. It looked like a child forcing a kitten's nose into a saucer of milk.

From *Dracula* by Bram Stoker

Look at the monsters below. How would you escape their clutches?

- Write the story of a fight between you and one of the monsters in the picture on page 24. Describe your struggle to survive.

- Follow these steps. You can use the sentence starters shown, or you can make up your own. Try to use at least **two** more sentences of your own each time.

1 You confront the monster:
   It was the ugliest sight I had ever seen...

2 Describe the monster's reaction to you:
   It gave a snarl of hate...

3 Describe your feelings:
   I could barely breathe, I was so frightened...

4 The monster attacks first:
   It gave a sudden terrible lunge...

5 Describe its strength:
   Its long fingers cut into my flesh and...

6 Describe how you fight back:
   I summoned all my strength to twist from its grip...

7 Describe how it fights back:
   Enraged, the monster...

8 Describe how you finally get the better of it:
   At that moment, I...

THE BEAST MUST DIE

Horror films and books usually end with the death of the monster. At the end of *Dracula,* the Count has been tracked back to his castle. He thinks he is safe, because night is about to fall:

The sun was almost down on the mountain top, and the shadows of the whole group fell long upon the snow. I saw the Count lying within the box upon the earth. He was deathly pale, just like a waxen image, and the red eyes glared with the horrible look I knew too well. As I looked, the eyes saw the sinking sun, and the look of hate in them turned to triumph.

But, on the instant, came the sweep and flash of Jonathan's great knife. I shrieked as I saw it shear through the throat; whilst at the same time Mr Morris's bowie knife plunged into the heart.

It was like a miracle; but before our eyes, and almost in the drawing of a breath, the whole body crumbled into dust and passed from our sight.

I shall be glad as long as I live that even in that moment of death there was in that face a look of peace, such as I never could have imagined.

From *Dracula* by Bram Stoker

In this original version, Dracula's head is cut off.

• Decide on a different death for Dracula. Four ideas are given here. You can use one of these, or perhaps you know another way of killing vampires.

Dracula is terrified of the sign of the cross. You chase him towards a windmill. Dracula turns to attack you. But he has not noticed the shape that the sails of the windmill make. The shape is a cross…

Vampires cannot survive in running water. You are chasing Dracula, but he tries to escape by crossing a river. The water is rough and you start to swim after the boat…

Dracula cannot survive in daylight. Instead he sleeps in a coffin during the day. But you manage to break through into the chamber where the coffin lies. You pull back the heavy curtains, letting in the light. Then you go towards the coffin…

Dracula can be killed with a stake through the heart. You corner Dracula in his castle. Dracula bares his teeth. You have no weapon. Then you notice a display of knives on the wall…

• Now write your own 'Death of Dracula'.

DESIGN YOUR OWN POSTER

Look closely at this poster of a film called 'Dracula'. Discuss these points with a partner.

1 What does the red writing make you think of?

2 Which words are made to stand out? Why?

3 What does the black background make you think of?

4 What expression can you see in Dracula's eyes?

5 What else do you notice about Dracula's face? How closely does this picture match Bram Stoker's description of Dracula on page 22?

6 What do you think about the girl? Is she frightened? Has she fainted? Or is she asleep?

Now design your own poster. Look at the pictures in this chapter to give you ideas. Follow these steps.

1 Choose the title of your film.

2 Choose the colours you will use.

3 Decide on the type of writing (font).

4 Decide on the actors and actresses you will use.

5 Try to think of a sub-title like 'Love Never Dies'.

6 Will the film be a U, PG, 12, 15 or 18?

HELP

Film Classifications

U = anyone can watch the film

PG = parents must decide if a child can watch the film

12 = only people 12 or over can watch the film

15 = only people 15 or over can watch the film

18 = only people 18 or over can watch the film

WHAT DID YOU LEARN?

In this unit you have looked at how horror stories are told.
Ask yourself how much you have learnt from this unit.
Answer the questions below.

1 Why do writers start horror stories with a mystery?

2 What is a cliffhanger?

3 Why do writers use cliffhangers?

4 Describe a suitable setting for a horror story.

5 How does a typical horror story end?

6 What kinds of details make a passage of horror more chilling?

7 What common features do monsters have?

HOW DID YOU DO?

1 Which part of this unit did you most enjoy?

2 In what ways is this work better than work you have done before?

3 If you had to go back to one section and do it again which one would you choose? Why?

4 What do you need to do to improve your own horror writing?

UNIT TWO

Newsroom

News is brought to us by television, radio and newspapers. In this unit you will look at how news stories are collected and presented.

You will develop your skills as:

SPEAKERS AND LISTENERS

by working as a news team and making decisions together
by reading a news bulletin

READERS

by finding information
by studying the news

WRITERS

by writing a newspaper article
by writing a script for a news bulletin

How does a story reach your newspaper pages? Turn the page to find out...

Look carefully at this picture of a newsroom.

Information can be beamed to the newsroom via satellite.

The editor decides which stories are used and where they go in the paper.

Journalists write their articles on word processors.

Some stories can be found on the Internet.

NEWS ON INTERNET

Some stories come in on tape.

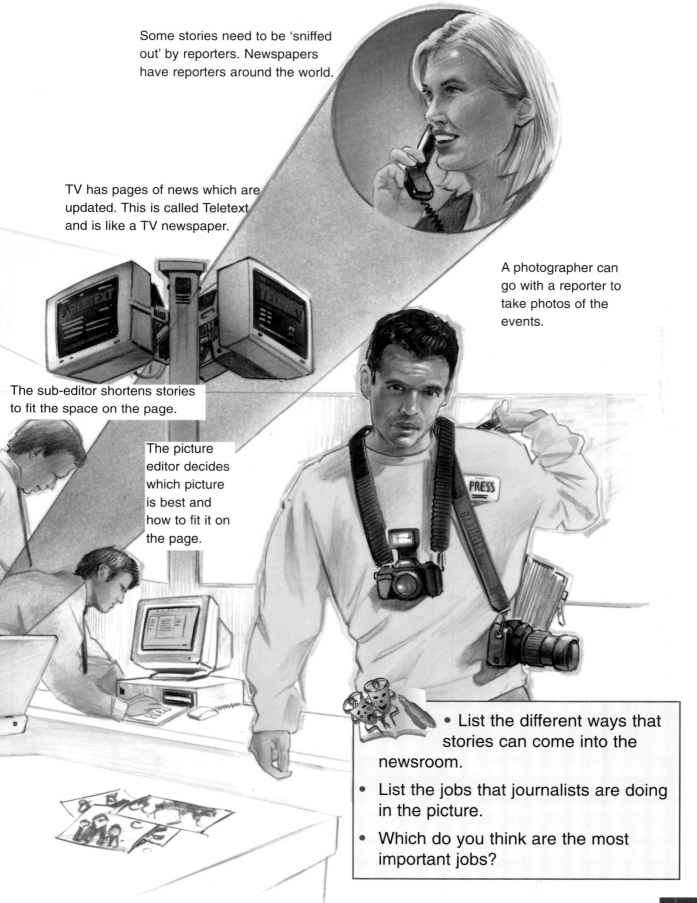

Some stories need to be 'sniffed out' by reporters. Newspapers have reporters around the world.

TV has pages of news which are updated. This is called Teletext and is like a TV newspaper.

A photographer can go with a reporter to take photos of the events.

The sub-editor shortens stories to fit the space on the page.

The picture editor decides which picture is best and how to fit it on the page.

• List the different ways that stories can come into the newsroom.

• List the jobs that journalists are doing in the picture.

• Which do you think are the most important jobs?

A STORY BREAKS

A lot of news pours into a newsroom. Decisions have to be made –
which news story is important and which is less important?

Reporter Carrie Ferrant is about to watch the late film when she gets a call from her Editor.

Carrie is sent to a fire at an old warehouse by the river.

Carrie goes to work finding out all the facts.

Can you tell me what you know ?

It started in the basement. It's nearly under control. 5 men have been taken to hospital.

She then talks to some witnesses. Outside Red Lion Pub.

RED LION

"We had to leave our house. We live too close to the warehouse.."

"We smelt the smoke about 1 o'clock."

Carrie phones in to the newsroom It is now 3.30 a.m.

Right I've typed it in. You get home and get some sleep!

Fire swept through the warehouse of Swan and Sons in the early hours of this morning. Twelve fire engines fought the blaze, which could be seen 20 miles away..

In the morning meeting

The Warehouse Fire. Have we got an angle on it ?

WHAT IS AN ANGLE?

An angle is a way of looking at a story. The story of the
warehouse fire could be looked at from several angles:

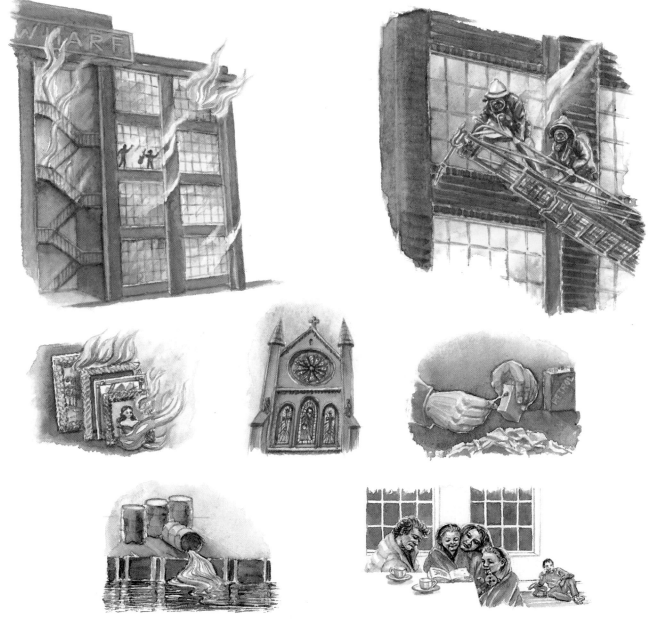

- the bravery of the fire-fighters
- the loss of precious paintings in the warehouse
- the possibility that the fire had been started on purpose (arson)
- the amazing survival of the church next door
- burning chemicals seeping into a nearby river
- people living near the fire spending the night in a nearby school

WHAT IS YOUR ANGLE?

- If you were Carrie which angle would you choose?
- Which angles do these headlines fit?

FIRE THREATENS ART TREASURES

BRAVE FIREFIGHTERS BEAT WAREHOUSE BLAZE

CITY FIRE: WAS IT DELIBERATE?

- Now write the headlines for the other angles.

BUT WILL IT MAKE THE FRONT PAGE?

Top stories are printed on the front page. Look at the front pages of newspapers.

- What makes a front page story?
- Why are other stories on the inside pages?
- Why do some funny stories appear on the front page?
- Look at different papers. Do papers have different sorts of headlines? Why?

WHAT ELSE HAVE WE GOT?

WELL, THERES A PLANE CRASH IN INDIA - 100 DEAD.

36hrs

A MAN IN SURREY HAS BROKEN THE RECORD FOR NON-STOP BARKING- 36 HOURS.

THERE'S THE BIG WAREHOUSE FIRE IN LONDON.

BOMB ALERT

A BOMB EXPLODED OUTSIDE BUCKINGHAM PALACE. QUEEN WASN'T HURT, BUT A ROYAL CORGI WAS KILLED.

AND AN OLD LADY FRIGHTENED AWAY A BURGULAR BY TRYING TO KISS HIM.

THE EDITOR MAKES A CLEAR DECISION

NOT THE WAREHOUSE FIRE.

- The editor chooses one serious story and one funny story to go on the front page. Which do you think he chooses?

LATER THAT DAY...

The morning edition of the newspaper has already been printed. But newspapers have later editions, to include news that happens later. Suddenly there is startling news from the warehouse. Part of the warehouse was used as a recording studio.

Now three bodies have been found in the smoking ruins. A famous band, The Sub-Zeroes, had been rehearsing in the building. No one has seen them since the fire.

ARE THE BODIES THOSE OF THE BAND?

Reporter Carrie Ferrant looks at her notebook. She talked to witnesses at the fire:

'Just before the fire I could hear music coming from the warehouse.' John Collins, 52, who had been drinking in the Red Lion opposite.

'We had a call at 11.43pm and responded as quickly as we could.' Arthur Morrison, firefighter.

'Thank God the church next door was untouched.' Alice Munro, whose flat overlooked the fire.

'We have no reason to believe anyone has been killed.' Jim Hardy, policeman.

'I did see some scruffy looking chaps in the pub. They looked a bit familiar, but I don't know much about pop groups! They went out together at about 10pm.' Landlady at the Red Lion.

'I couldn't hear anything from the warehouse at all. No. I can't remember if I was wearing my hearing aid, to be honest with you.' Sid Chesterman, 70, who lives near the warehouse.

CARRIE'S NOTES

Carrie made notes about the facts:

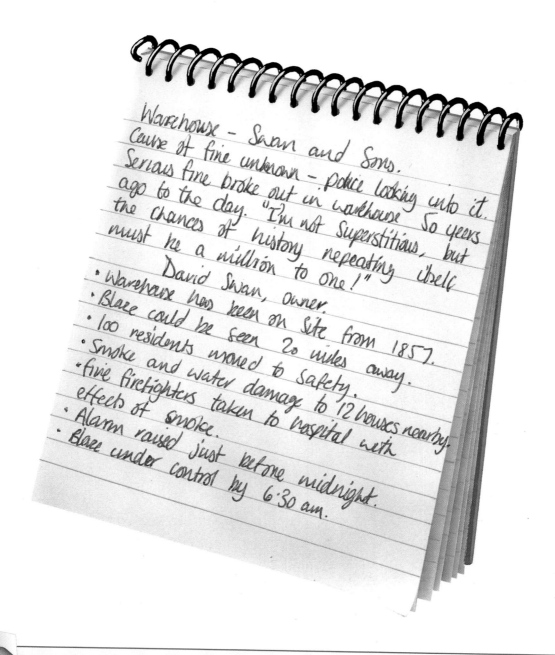

Warehouse – Swan and Sons.
Cause of fire unknown – police looking into it.
Serious fire broke out in warehouse 50 years
ago to the day. "I'm not superstitious, but
the chances of history repeating itself
must be a million to one!"
David Swan, owner.
• Warehouse has been on site from 1857.
• Blaze could be seen 20 miles away.
• 100 residents moved to safety.
• Smoke and water damage to 12 houses nearby.
• Five firefighters taken to hospital with
effects of smoke.
• Alarm raised just before midnight.
• Blaze under control by 6:30 am.

- What angle should Carrie take on the story?
- Does she have enough information to take an angle on the band?
- What other useful information can she use?

PICTURE POWER

A picture is worth a thousand words.

• Choose the pictures that you think the following papers would use:

 – a pop magazine

 – a local paper

 – a national daily.

HEADLINES

Here are some headlines that you could use for your story, or you can make up your own.

THREE DEAD IN WAREHOUSE FIRE

MYSTERY DEATHS IN CITY FIRE

ROCK BAND IN FIRE TRAGEDY?

THREE BODIES FOUND IN GUTTED WAREHOUSE

ROCK LEGENDS DEAD?

ARSON ATTACK CLAIMS THREE LIVES

• Now write the warehouse fire story to go with your headline. Here are some ideas to get you started.

Fears were growing last night that...
The fire broke out at...
An eye-witness at the scene said that...
Tearful fans gathered to...
Tonight police are asking...

LAYOUT

- Look at this page from a newspaper. Match the arrows with the correct terms from the Help Box on page 43.

THE SENTINEL

NO. 10,181   **2 SEPTEMBER 1998**   50p

MP BACKS CUTS TO NHS BUDGET   ?

Plans Revealed   ?

? → *Nurses are under increasing pressure*

?

Special Report
p6

Arts and Books
p10

TV and Radio
p30

Weather and Sport
p32

?

HELP

Headline:

- The title of the story
- Large type
- Gives the most important fact of the story

Subheading:

- Under the headline
- Gives more information about the story
- Type is smaller than headline

Article:

- The story
- Printed in columns
- Small print

Column:

- Rows of print that run down the page

Caption:

- Line of print under the photograph
- Explains what is in the photograph

- Design the front page of your own newspaper to show how the headline, pictures and story would appear.

WRITING THE NEWS

You have seen that news has to be put in a certain order in a newspaper. The same is true of television news. The only difference is that we see and hear the reporter talking to the camera.
Do you think you can read the news?

> • Write a television or radio news bulletin based on stories from nursery rhymes. Try to write at least three different stories, based on nursery rhymes such as:
>
> The Old Woman who lived in a Shoe
>
> Three Blind Mice
>
> Jack and Jill
>
> Sing a Song of Sixpence
>
> Look at the examples opposite to give you ideas.

Humpty Dumpty sat on a wall
Humpty Dumpty had a great fall
All the King's Horses and all the King's Men
Couldn't put Humpty together again.

HUMPTY IN DEATH PLUNGE

Humpty Dumpty fell from a 40 foot wall today. The King's Horses and Men who were in the area tried to put the badly injured egg-man Humpty back together, but could not. He was taken to Wallsend Hospital but doctors said he was dead on arrival. Was it a tragic accident – or did he fall, or worse, was he pushed?

Hey diddle, diddle
The cat and the fiddle
The cow jumped over the moon;
The little dog laughed to see such sport
And the dish ran away with the spoon.

COW IN ORBIT

Experts last night were trying to work out the biggest space mystery ever. How did a cow get into outer space? And when it reached the moon how did it jump over? Possible links are being made with the strange theft of a spoon back on Earth. Last night a corgi called Rex was helping police with their enquiries.

UNSCRAMBLING THE NEWS

The six news stories opposite have been chosen for a TV
news programme for teenage viewers. They are in the wrong
order – can you put them in the right order?

HELP

There are two types of news stories – hard and soft.

Hard news

- news stories that are just 'breaking'
- about important events

Soft news

- about less important events
- not urgent
- funny stories

Hard news goes before soft news. Can you see why?

- There is one soft news story among the six in the list.
  Which is it? Where would you place it?

- There are five hard news stories. The most important story will
  go first, the next most important second, and so on. Work out
  your own running order.

- If you had 20 minutes for the programme, how would you
  divide up the time? Work out the number of minutes you would
  give to each story.

1   A huge banner painted by thousands of children from all over the world has been put on show in Ireland. The banner is a mile and half long. It tells the sad story of Korky the Killer Whale. People who are fond of animals want Korky released back into the wild.

2   England footballer Stuart Pearce has resigned as manager of Nottingham Forest. The decision comes after Forest were relegated from the Premier League. However, Pearce has said he'll continue to play for the team.

3   Three bodies found after a fire in an old warehouse have led to tearful scenes. Fans of The Sub-Zeroes fear the bodies may be those of the band. The group used the warehouse as a studio. The cause of the fire is still not known. Police have asked anyone with information to come forward.

4   Going to the dentist is something people dread. But fillings could be a thing of the past thanks to a new invention – a tablet that you don't even have to swallow. But Dr David Ball says that people should continue to brush their teeth well. The drug is still being tested.

5   American pilot Linda Finch has reached Australia. She is following the path of Amelia Erhart, who disappeared 60 years ago when trying to fly round the world. Linda Finch is even flying the same kind of plane as Erhart.

6   The African children who have lost their mothers and fathers. Aid workers are working night and day to cope with children who are returning home to Rwanda. Three years ago thousands of families fled from Rwanda when war broke out. Around ten thousand children have no parents to go home to.

LINKS

Link sentences help news-readers to move from one story to the next. Here are some links from a news programme:

Hello, and first...

Next we move on to...

Sports fans will be interested to hear that...

Finally...

- Put each of these links before the story (on page 47) it leads into.
- Make up two more links to complete your bulletin.

DID YOU GET IT RIGHT?

Now look at the running order and times on page 55.

- Discuss anything which surprises you. Can you explain why the times are so different for each story?
- The news programme is aimed at your age group. How many of these stories would you expect to see on the adult news on the same day?

READING THE NEWS

Could you be a news-reader? Have a go at using the script you have written to see if you could be a presenter. You could use a video camera to record your performance and then see how good you were.

HELP

What you need

- a table and chair
- the script with links written in
- a video camera
- someone to read the news
- someone to film the news

Tips for the news-reader

- Look at the camera as often as possible.
- Hold your script at an angle, not flat on the table.
- Read in a clear, normal voice.
- Take your time.
- Practise a few times.

- What do you think makes a good news-reader?

HIJACK! THE CASE OF THE MISSING BUS

You are a TV reporter and this is your big chance.

A school bus has gone missing on its way to summer camp in Scotland, close to where you live. It was last seen near Lago, a small town.

You call the Headteacher.

John Grant here... What? Yes, that's our bus... How many?... 42 children and three staff... Year 9... Yes, three members of staff... Where were they going?... They were going to Glebelands summer camp for a week... No, we've had no ransom demand. I can't believe there's a problem... It's probably just a silly mistake of some kind... No, I couldn't say what kind of mistake.

HEAD TEACHER

GETTING THE FACTS

You interview local people.

They filled up with petrol about half past ten... Then they drove off... Yeah, the bus stopped, and I think the brown van was in front. I couldn't see much from here. I thought maybe it was another teacher who had caught up with them for some reason.

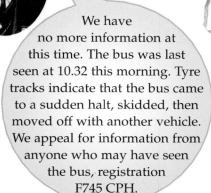

We have no more information at this time. The bus was last seen at 10.32 this morning. Tyre tracks indicate that the bus came to a sudden halt, skidded, then moved off with another vehicle. We appeal for information from anyone who may have seen the bus, registration F745 CPH.

Some kids did come in. I clearly remember several had a Coke. They were nice kids. I'm sorry if they have been kidnapped.

- Now put together the information for your first report. It must take exactly one minute to read aloud.

- You can use some of these sentence openings or make up your own.

A school bus has...

It was reported missing after failing to turn up at...

Shortly before disappearing, the bus stopped...

It was last seen near...

Petrol pump attendant Joe Walker told us...

Tyre tracks in the road show that...

Headteacher Mr John Grant told us that...

In the bus were... from...

The policeman, who is in charge of the case, appealed...

The bus registration is...

This is... reporting from...

- Record your report on tape or read it aloud to the class.

TWO HOURS LATER...

It is time for the next news bulletin.

What do we know about 'Free The Children'?

This is a message from 'Free The Children'. We believe this country should be free from laws. We believe every person has the right to make up their own mind how they want to live their lives. We do not believe children should be forced to attend school. Schools are prisons. Children should be free to live their lives the way they want. The children of Sackville High have been liberated by us. We demand that this tape be played on radio stations throughout the country. Only when our demands are met will the children be released...

Hmm... leader is a man called Jude Evans. Had a bad time at school, doesn't want other kids to have to put up with the same thing. He tried the same thing two years ago, but he gave himself up, and got two years in prison... came out just last month.

Well, I saw this big bus and this brown van in the wood. I couldn't see too well, but I think he had a red shirt. Yes, the guy in the red shirt nailed something to a tree. I don't know what. There was a girl too, in a big blue anorak, looked like she was with him. I didn't see any kids...

I know no more than you do. Everything possible is being done. We have a hundred officers on the case. We appeal to the kidnappers to return the children to their parents...

Will we broadcast their demands? I can't say. I'll have to speak to Mrs Owens, who owns the station...

• You need to update your story. You can use some of these sentence openings or make up your own.

There has been an amazing new development...

It now seems that the bus was taken by...

'Free the Children' is run by..., who...

The kidnappers are demanding that...

Two years ago...

'Free the Children' believes...

Police say...

This is... reporting from...

• Record your new report on tape or read it aloud to the class.

SHOWDOWN!

- Get into groups of three.

- This is a timed activity. You have 15 minutes to get ready for your bulletin. Start timing yourself **now**.

- Look at the picture and make notes for your bulletin.

  1 What is happening?

  2 Where is the bus exactly?

  3 Why has it stopped?

  4 What are the police marksmen doing?

  5 What is the police chief saying? (You must make this up.)

  6 Who is driving the bus?

  7 What can you see in the bus?

- Decide who will read the bulletin and help them to rehearse.

- You might start:
  The Sackville School bus hijack is reaching a dramatic climax...

- Now record your third report.

- Listen to each group's report and say what was good about it.

AND NEXT...

What do you think will happen next in the story?

- Will the hijackers give in?
- Will they make demands?
- Will they make threats?
- Will they say why they are doing it?
- Will the police be allowed to help the teachers and children by bringing food and drink?
- If they do, who will take it into the bus?
- What will the police chief be saying in half an hour's time?

- Will the head of Sackville School arrive and make a statement?
- Who else might get involved?
- Will more police arrive?
- Will any children be seen?
- Will there be talks?
- Will the second hijacker be seen?
- How will the atmosphere change?

- Use the questions above to help you to decide what happens next.
- Make notes on your ideas.
- Make up what people such as the police chief say. Add this to your notes.
- Use your notes to write a final bulletin.

Original running order for 'Unscrambling the news'

Rwandan children separated from parents (six minutes)

Warehouse mystery deaths (three minutes)

Korky the Whale banner in Ireland (one minute)

Stuart Pearce resignation (two minutes)

Linda Finch round-the-world flight (four minutes)

Tooth decay report (four minutes)

HOW DID YOU DO?

You have read a lot about how news is collected and presented. To find out how much you have learnt from this unit, complete the tasks below.

1 List two ways that news arrives in the newsroom.

2 Describe what happens to a story after the reporter sends it into the newsroom. Set your work out like this:

Reporter sends story

It is typed into the word processor

(Now continue)

3 Explain what the editor and sub-editor do.

4 List three other jobs in the newsroom.

5 Explain what an 'angle' on a story is.

6 Explain the difference between hard and soft news.

7 Say where hard and soft news go in a newspaper or a news bulletin.

8 Write down the correct terms for the layout of a front page.

9 Give an example of a link between news stories.

10 Write down three or four rules for a good news-reader.

UNIT THREE

Macbeth

In this unit you will study Shakespeare's play *Macbeth*. You will get to know the plot and think about why the characters behave as they do. You will also be introduced to Shakespeare's language. As you work through this unit you will develop your skills as:

SPEAKERS AND LISTENERS

by taking part in role play
by discussing the themes
by discussing characters

READERS

by reading some of the text as Shakespeare wrote it
by watching key scenes from the play
by finding evidence for your ideas

WRITERS

by writing for different purposes
by organising your ideas into a longer piece of writing

Turn the page to begin thinking about some of the themes in *Macbeth*…

AN INTRODUCTION TO THE MAIN THEMES OF THE PLAY

ROLE PLAY CARDS

Use these role play cards to explore some of the themes and issues you will come across in the play *Macbeth*. When you get your card, read through the notes and discuss them with your group. Then role play what is happening. It is better to improvise (make it up as you go along) so there is no need to write a script.

ROLE CARD A (GROUP OF 2)

Your character

You are very superstitious. You always read your horoscope. You have even been to a fortune teller.

What's happening

Your friend really wants you to go out to see a film. The film's called *Out of the Blue*. It is on for one night only. Your horoscope said to stay away from the colour blue all that day.

Act out your conversation.

ROLE CARD B (GROUP OF 4/5)

Your character

You like to be with your mates. You often meet up with them on a Saturday to go into town. Recently they've been talking about shop-lifting. You think some of your mates may have done this already.

What's happening

Your mates point out something in a shop. They dare you to shop-lift it. They tell you it's easy but you're not so sure. They try to persuade you.

Act out your conversation. Do you decide to do what they tell you, or not?

ROLE CARD C (GROUP OF 3)

Your character
Everyone at school has trendy new pencil cases. You're fed up with being the odd one out. You take some money from your mum's purse so you can have one too.

What's happening
You arrive home from school to find both your parents waiting for you and they are not pleased. You try to explain why you took the money.
Act out your conversation.

ROLE CARD D (GROUP OF 2)

Your character
You've been going out with your boy/girlfriend for some time but have always dreamt of being famous.

What's happening
You have just had a letter offering you a place at stage school. You are very keen, but it means moving away. Your boy/girlfriend doesn't want you to go. Act out the conversation in which your boy/girlfriend tries to make you stay.

Each role play card introduces a problem that can arise.

• Role play the situation and show the other groups what is happening.

• Invite the rest of the class to talk about what happened in your role play.

Did the characters do the right thing?

Are there any other solutions to the problem?

• What did you notice about how different people tried to **persuade** others to do something?

HOW AMBITIOUS ARE YOU?

AMBITION
To have an ambition means that there is something you really want to achieve.

AMBITIOUS
To be ambitious means that you really want to be successful.

With a partner:

- Choose three of your ambitions.

- Talk about what you would have to do to achieve these things.

- If you knew something about the future, how would it make you feel?

- Imagine a fortune teller has just told you that you will be a famous sports person. How would it make you feel? Would it change your life?

- Have a go at **predicting** some things which might happen to others in your class.

HELP

Predicting means being able to guess what might happen in the future.

...to travel the world

...to play for England

...to own an expensive car

...to rule a country

...to win the lottery

...to be famous

ACT 1 SCENE 1 – THE WITCHES

The opening of Shakespeare's play is very **dramatic.** Three witches open the play. They meet in a 'desolate place'. They arrange to meet Macbeth after a battle.

> **Dramatic** means 'sudden', 'striking' or 'impressive'. Here the opening of the play is designed to grab your attention.

A desolate place. Thunder and lightning. Enter three WITCHES

FIRST WITCH	When shall we three meet again?
	In thunder, lightning, or in rain?
SECOND WITCH	When the hurly-burly's done,
	When the battle's lost, and won.
THIRD WITCH	That will be ere the set of sun.
FIRST WITCH	Where the place?
SECOND WITCH	Upon the heath.
THIRD WITCH	There to meet with Macbeth.
FIRST WITCH	I come, Graymalkin.
SECOND WITCH	Paddock calls.
THIRD WITCH	Anon.
ALL	Fair is foul, and foul is fair,
	Hover through the fog and filthy air.

Act 1, Scene 1

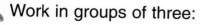

Work in groups of three:

- Read through the lines a few times.
- Try saying the lines in different ways:
  shout whisper speak quickly speak slowly.
  Listen carefully to the words. How do they sound?
  What differences do you notice about each way of saying them?

READING THE PLAY

The play is split into five parts. Each part is called an Act.

You are going to carry on looking at Act 1. Read the cartoon below.

THE KING HEARS OF THE BRAVERY OF MACBETH AND BANQUO, WHO HAVE WON THE BATTLE.

ON THEIR WAY TO MEET THE KING, MACBETH AND BANQUO ARE STOPPED BY THREE WITCHES WHO PREDICT THEIR FUTURES.

HAIL MACBETH, THANE OF GLAMIS!

ALL HAIL MACBETH THANE OF CAWDOR...

...THAT SHALT BE KING HEREAFTER

THEY ALSO TELL BANQUO THAT HIS CHILDREN WILL BE KINGS.

ROSS ARRIVES WITH NEWS THAT KING DUNCAN HAS MADE MACBETH 'THANE OF CAWDOR'.

TWO TRUTHS ARE TOLD...

IN ORDER FOR THE THIRD PREDICTION TO COME TRUE, MACBETH WOULD HAVE TO KILL KING DUNCAN.

MACBETH TELLS HIS WIFE ABOUT THE WITCHES IN A LETTER. SHE WORRIES THAT HER HUSBAND IS TOO DECENT TO CARRY OUT THE MURDER.

YET DO I FEAR THY NATURE, IT IS TOO FULL O' TH' MILK OF HUMAN KINDNESS.

THAT NIGHT KING DUNCAN ARRIVES AT MACBETH'S CASTLE, AND IS WELCOMED BY LADY MACBETH.

IF WE SHOULD FAIL?

WE FAIL!

MACBETH TRIES TO PREPARE HIMSELF FOR THE MURDER. IT IS LADY MACBETH WHO FINALLY PERSUADES HIM TO GO AHEAD WITH IT.

- Try to watch a film of Act 1.
- Now read some of Act 1 as Shakespeare wrote it.

THE ART OF PERSUASION

Macbeth's castle, near the Great Hall. Music and torches. Enter a butler and many servants with dishes and service over the stage. Then enter MACBETH

MACBETH   If it were done when 'tis done, then 'twere well
                It were done quickly; if th'assassination
                Could trammel up the consequence, and catch
                With his surcease, success; that but this blow
                Might be the be-all and the end-all – here,
                But here, upon this bank and shoal of time,
                We'd jump the life to come. But in these cases,
                We still have judgement here; that we but teach
                Bloody instructions, which being taught, return
                To plague th'inventor; this even-handed justice
                Commends th'ingredients of our poisoned chalice
                To our own lips. He's here in double trust:
                First, as I am his kinsman and his subject,
                Strong both against the deed; then, as his host,
                Who should against his murderer shut the door,
                Not bear the knife myself. Besides, this Duncan
                Hath borne his faculties so meek, hath been
                So clear in his great office, that his virtues
                Will plead like angles, trumpet-tongu'd against
                The deep damnation of his taking-off;
                And pity, like a naked newborn babe
                Striding the blast, or heaven's cherubin hors'd
                Upon the sightless couriers of the air,
                Shall blow the horrid deed in every eye,
                That tears shall drown the wind. I have no spur
                To prick the sides of my intent, but only
                Vaulting ambition which o'erleaps itself
                And falls on the other –

                                              Act 1, Scene 7

In the scene you have just read, Macbeth speaks aloud his thoughts about the murder. He wants to be king, but he doubts whether he should kill King Duncan.

Below is a list of Macbeth's arguments. Next to the arguments are lines from Macbeth's speech.

I will be killed if caught	*I am ... his subject,* *Strong both against the deed*
I am a relative of the King	*Duncan* *Hath borne his faculties so meek, hath been* *So clear in his great office*
I am his subject and should be loyal to the King	*I have no spur* *To prick the sides of my intent, but only* *Vaulting ambition*
I am his host and I should protect my guest	*This even-handed justice* *Commends th'ingredients of our poisoned* *chalice* *To our own lips*
Duncan is a good King with good qualities	*I am ... his host,* *Who should against his murderer* *shut the door*
I will be damned in heaven	*I am his kinsman*
I am very ambitious	*his virtues* *Will plead like angels, trumpet-tongu'd against* *The deep damnation of his taking-off.*

- Match the lines in the play to the arguments.
- Which ones are for murder?
- Which ones are against murder?
- What do you think Macbeth will do?

Lady Macbeth is more determined at this point. She persuades her husband to go ahead with their plan to murder Duncan. Macbeth says 'We will proceed no further in this business.' But by the end of the scene he has changed his mind…

- Look at the lines below. Translate them into modern English using grids like these. The first ones have been done for you.

Macbeth	Modern Meaning
We will proceed no further in this business	We will not carry out our plans to murder the King
I dare do all that become a man; Who dares do more is none	
If we should fail?	

Lady Macbeth	Modern Meaning
Was hope drunk? Art thou afeard?	Have you lost your nerve?
What beast was't, then, That made you break this enterprise to me?	
We fail! But screw your courage to the sticking-place, And we'll not fail.	

- Look at this conversation between Macbeth and Lady Macbeth. What are the details of their plan?
- How does Lady Macbeth persuade Macbeth to kill the King?

- Imagine you are directing the play. Explain to the actress playing the part of Lady Macbeth how she should persuade her husband. Write down five points you would make.

MACBETH   If we should fail?

LADY MACBETH   We fail!
But screw your courage to the sticking-place,
And we'll not fail. When Duncan is asleep –
Whereto the rather shall his day's hard journey
Soundly invite him – his two chamberlains
Will I with wine and wassail so convince
That memory, the warder of the brain,
Shall be a fume, and the receipt of reason
A limbeck only: when in swinish sleep
Their drenched natures lie as in a death,
What cannot you and I perform upon
The unguarded Duncan? What not put upon
His spongy officers, who shall bear the guilt
Of our great quell?

MACBETH   Bring forth men-children only;
For thy undaunted mettle should compose
Nothing but males. Will it not be received,
When we have mark'd with blood those sleepy two
Of his own chamber and used their very daggers,
That they have done't?

LADY MACBETH   Who dares receive it other,
As we shall make our griefs and clamour roar
Upon his death?

MACBETH   I am settled, and bend up
Each corporal agent to this terrible feat.
Away, and mock the time with fairest show:
False face must hide what the false heart doth know.

Act 1, scene 7

ACT 2

MURDER

You have been called to investigate a crime – the murder of King Duncan.

- In groups draw up a list of suspects to be interviewed.

- Decide who will do the interviewing and who will be interviewed.

- Decide on the questions to be asked. (Remember to pretend you don't know who did it!)

- Use the table below to help you set the scene.

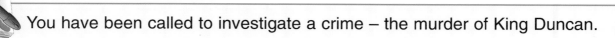

Who has been murdered?		
Who was in the castle at the time?		
Suspect	*Possible motives?*	*Evidence?*

In role play:

- Act out one or two of your interviews.
  Remember Lady Macbeth and Macbeth are lying.

Now write a police report of your investigation. Use a copy of the sheet below.

Police investigation by _____

Crime _____

Suspect _____

Scene of the crime _____

Findings _____

_____

_____

_____

_____

_____

_____

_____

_____

_____

_____

Conclusion _____

_____

_____

Signature _____

ACT 3

A ghost plays an important part in Act 3, Scene 4. He has a
dramatic effect on Macbeth's behaviour.

MACBETH, NOW KING, INVITES BANQUO TO A BANQUET THAT EVENING. BANQUO IS SUSPICIOUS AND MACBETH FEARS HIM.

THOU HAST IT NOW, KING, CAWDOR, GLAMIS, ALL.

FAIL NOT OUR FEAST

UNKNOWN TO LADY MACBETH, MACBETH GIVES INSTRUCTIONS TO HAVE BANQUO AND HIS SON MURDERED.

BOTH OF YOU KNOW BANQUO WAS YOUR ENEMY

LADY MACBETH NOTICES HER HUSBAND'S TROUBLED MIND AND TRIES TO CALM HIM.

O, FULL OF SCORPIONS IS MY MIND, DEAR WIFE!

WHAT'S DONE IS DONE

BANQUO IS MURDERED, BUT HIS SON, FLEANCE ESCAPES..

FLY, GOOD FLEANCE, FLY, FLY, FLY!

THE TABLE'S FULL!

AT THE BANQUET IN THE PALACE THAT NIGHT, MACBETH IS HAUNTED BY THE GHOST OF BANQUO, AND ALL THE GUESTS NOTICE HIS STRANGE BEHAVIOUR.

LADY MACBETH TRIES TO CALM HER HUSBAND AND EXCUSE HIS BEHAVIOUR. MACBETH SAYS HE WILL VISIT THE WITCHES AGAIN.

I WILL TOMORROW —TO THE WEIRD SISTERS

MY FRIENDS...

- Who is the ghost?
  - Why is Macbeth so frightened of the ghost?
- How does Macbeth behave?
- If the ghost could speak, what do you think it would tell the guests?

- Complete the ghost's speech to the guests.
- Would you have an actor on stage as Banquo's ghost? Or would you have an empty space at the table? Which is the best solution? Why?

A WITCH'S SPELL

In Act 4, Scene 1 the witches brew a spell. The spell is to show Macbeth the future. Their spell is made up of some *very* strange ingredients!

A desolate place near Forres. Thunder. Enter the three WITCHES

FIRST WITCH
Thrice the brindled cat hath mewed.

SECOND WITCH
Thrice and once the hedge-pig whined.

THIRD WITCH
Harpier cries, ''Tis time, 'tis time.'

FIRST WITCH
Round about the cauldron go;
In the poisoned entrails throw.
Toad, that under cold stone
Days and nights has thirty-one
Sweltered venom sleeping got,
Boil thou first i'th'charmed pot.

ALL
Double, double, toil and trouble;
Fire burn, and cauldron bubble.

SECOND WITCH
Fillet of a fenny snake,
In the cauldron boil and bake:
Eye of newt, and toe of frog,
Wool of bat, and tongue of dog,
Adder's fork, and blind-worm's sting,
Lizard's leg, and howlet's wing,
For a charm of powerful trouble,
Like a hell-broth, boil and bubble.

ALL
Double, double, toil and trouble,
Fire burn, and cauldron bubble.

THIRD WITCH
Scale of dragon, tooth of wolf,
Witches' mummy, maw and gulf
Of the ravined salt-sea shark,
Root of hemlock, digged i'th'dark;
Liver of blaspheming Jew,
Gall of goat, and slips of yew
Silvered in the moon's eclipse;
Nose of Turk, and Tartar's lips,
Finger of birth-strangled babe,
Ditch-delivered by a drab,
Make the gruel thick and slab.
Add thereto a tiger's chawdron
For th'ingredience of our cauldron.

ALL
Double, double, toil and trouble,
Fire burn, and cauldron bubble.

SECOND WITCH
Cool it with a baboon's blood,
Then the charm is firm and good.

Act 4, Scene 1

• Copy the cauldron below. Draw and label all the ingredients of the witches' spell. You may need to look up some of the words in a dictionary.

• Invent your own spell written in rhyming couplets.
Try to write at least *eight* lines

HELP

Rhyming couplets

Rhyming couplets are made when each pair of lines rhymes, for example:

Eye of newt, and toe of frog,

Wool of bat, and tongue of dog,

Adder's fork, and blind-worm's sting,

Lizard's leg, and howlet's wing,

Each pair of lines is called a **couplet** (from the word 'couple').

For your spell, you could use modern ingredients or think of different creatures.

Write a list of ingredients first. Then choose ones that rhyme.

ACT 4

The witches give Macbeth a glimpse of the future.

They also give him three more predictions.

Read the cartoon below, then discuss these questions in pairs:

1 How do you think Macbeth feels after hearing the three predictions?

2 Why do you think Macbeth decides to kill Macduff's family. After all, they are no threat to him.

3 How much has Macbeth changed since we first met him? He was described as 'brave Macbeth' at the start of the play. How would you describe him now?

MACBETH VISITS THE WITCHES WHO SHOW HIM APPARITIONS, WHO SPEAK TO HIM...

'BEWARE MACDUFF...'

'... NONE OF WOMAN BORN SHALL HARM MACBETH...'

'... MACBETH SHALL NEVER VANQUISHED BE UNTIL GREAT BIRNAM WOOD TO HIGH DUNSINANE SHALL COME AGAINST HIM...'

MACBETH IS TOLD THAT MACDUFF HAS FLED TO ENGLAND. HE DECIDES TO KILL EVERY MEMBER OF MACDUFF'S FAMILY.

IN ENGLAND, MACDUFF AND MALCOLM DISCUSS MACBETH. ROSS ARRIVES TO TELL MACDUFF THAT HIS WIFE AND CHILDREN HAVE BEEN MURDERED AND HIS CASTLE SEIZED

YOUR CASTLE IS SURPRISED, YOUR WIFE AND BABES SAVAGELY SLAUGHTERED!

THEY PLAN TO GATHER AN ARMY AGAINST MACBETH.

ACT 5

OUT, DAMNED SPOT...

LADY MACBETH IS NOW SERIOUSLY DISTURBED BY ALL THAT HAS HAPPENED. SHE IS FOUND SLEEPWALKING, TRYING TO WASH IMAGINARY SPOTS OF BLOOD FROM HER HANDS.

A LARGE ARMY IS GATHERING NEARBY. MALCOLM GIVES ORDERS THAT EVERY SOLDIER MUST CUT DOWN A BRANCH SO MACBETH CANNOT TELL THEIR NUMBERS.

AT DUNSINANE CASTLE...

THE QUEEN, MY LORD, IS DEAD!

METHOUGHT THE WOOD BEGAN TO MOVE!

MACBETH IS TOLD THAT LADY MACBETH IS DEAD. HE STILL THINKS HE CANNOT BE CONQUERED, BUT IS THEN TOLD THAT BIRNAM WOOD IS MOVING

EVENTUALLY MACBETH AND MACDUFF FIGHT. MACBETH REALISES HIS MISTAKES WHEN MACDUFF TELLS HIM HE WAS BORN BY CAESAREAN.

MACDUFF KILLS MACBETH AND CUTS OFF HIS HEAD.

MALCOLM IS HAILED THE NEW KING OF SCOTLAND.

Ross has to tell Macduff what has happened to his family. He delays in telling him – why might that be? Think about how you would break some bad news to a friend.

- Write your own script of the conversation between Ross and Macduff.

- What do you think Ross would say to Macduff about the death of his wife and son?

- Now act out your script with a partner.

PREDICTIONS

The witches predict the following things:

1 Macbeth will be Thane of Cawdor

2 Macbeth will become King

3 Macbeth should beware Macduff

4 Nobody 'of woman born shall harm Macbeth'

5 Macbeth will never be defeated until Burnham Wood comes to 'High Dunsinane Hill'.

- How have predictions 3, 4 and 5 become true?

- How does Macbeth react when he finds out that predictions 4 and 5 are true?

THE WOOD COMES TO DUNSINANE

Read this passage from Act 5.

Enter a Messenger.

MACB. Thou comest to use they tongue; thy story quickly.

MESS. Gracious my lord,
I should report that which I say I saw,
But know not how to do it.

MACB. Well, say, sir.

MESS. As I did stand my watch upon the hill,
I look'd toward Birnam, and anon, methought,
The wood began to move.

MACB. Liar and slave!

MESS. Let me endure your wrath, if 't be not so:
Within this three mile may you see it coming;
I say, a moving grove.

MACB. If thou speak'st false,
Upon the next tree shalt thou hang alive,
Till famine cling thee: if thy speech be sooth,
I care not if thou dost for me as much.

I pull in resolution, and begin
To doubt the equivocation of the fiend
That lies like truth: 'Fear not, till Birnam wood
Do come to Dunsinane': and now a wood
Comes toward Dunsinane. Arm, arm, and out!
If this which he avouches does appear,
There is no flying hence nor tarrying here.
I 'gin to be aweary of the sun,
And wish the estate o' the world were now undone.
Ring the alarum-bell! Blow, wind! come, wrack!
At least we'll die with harness on our back.

Act 5, Scene 5

- How is Macbeth feeling here? Is he
  – confident
  – brave
  – fearful?

MACBETH FIGHTS MACDUFF

They fight.

MACBETH
                           Thou losest labour:
As easy mayst thou the intrenchant air
With thy keen sword impress as make me bleed:
Let fall thy blade on vulnerable crests:
I bear a charmed life, which must not yield
To one of woman born.

MACDUFF
                            Despair thy charm;
And let the angel whom thou still hast served
Tell thee, Macduff was from his mother's womb
Untimely ripp'd.

MACBETH
Accursed be that tongue that tells me so,
For it hath cow'd my better part of man!
And be these juggling fiends no more believed,
That palter with us in a double sense;
That keep the word of promise to our ear,
And break it to our hope. I'll not fight with thee.

MACDUFF
Then yield thee, coward.

Act 5, Scene 8

- Do you think Macbeth knows his luck has finally run out? Find the line where he seems to give up.

- Read on to line 34, 'And damn'd be him that first cries, 'Hold, enough!''. Why doesn't Macbeth give in? Why does he decide to die fighting?

- What do you think of this decision? Do you admire him or not?

You have watched the whole play. You have worked on the activities in the first part of this unit. Use the 'Focus On Sheets' on the following pages to look at some of the characters more closely.

You could split into groups to look at different characters and then report back.

FOCUS ON MACBETH

Derek Jacobi as Macbeth, RSC, 1993

- What crimes does Macbeth commit during the play?

- Look at the list of words below which are used in the play to describe Macbeth (use a dictionary if you are not sure of their meanings). Which do you agree with? Which don't you agree with? Why?

brave	avaricious	wicked	mad
tyrant	false	devilish	hell hound
black	deceitful	fiend	coward
devil	malicious	monster	butcher

- How does the character of Macbeth change throughout the play? On a separate sheet, copy the graph below. Fill it in to show how Macbeth's fortunes and character change. Use some of the adjectives from the list above. It has been started for you:

brave

weak

deceitful

• Put the following events into order to show what happens to Macbeth.

1 Macbeth murders King Duncan

2 He arranges the murder of Lady Macduff and her children

3 He wins the battle and is honoured by King Duncan

4 Macbeth prepares for battle. He is told the Queen is dead and Birnam Wood moves

5 Macbeth is crowned King of Scotland

6 He meets the three witches

7 He arranges Banquo's murder

8 He is beheaded by Macduff

9 He revisits the three witches

10 Macbeth fights Macduff and believes he cannot be harmed

11 He sees Banquo's ghost

• Match these lines from the play with the events above.

A For brave Macbeth – well he deserves that name

B I will tomorrow to the weird sisters

C Banquo, thy soul's flight, if it hid Heaven, must find it out tonight

D The sovereignty will fall upon Macbeth

E Behold where stands th' usurper's cursed head

F All hail, Macbeth, that shalt be King hereafter

G I have done the deed

H Give to th' edge o' th' sword his wife, his babes

I I bear a charmed life which must not yield to one of woman born

J The table's full

K The Queen, my Lord, is dead

FOCUS ON LADY MACBETH

At the end of Act 2

Lady Macbeth persuades her husband, Macbeth, to carry out the murder of King Duncan.

- What sort of person is she?
- How would you describe her relationship with Macbeth?
- How does she react to the murder?

At the end of Act 3

- Which of the words below best describe Lady Macbeth?

  ambitious   persuasive

  in charge   brave

  ruthless   clever

- Can you think of any other words to describe Lady Macbeth?
- Can you find any extracts in the play which support your view of Lady Macbeth?

Cheryl Campbell as Lady Macbeth, RSC, 1993

At the end of Act 5

- Lady Macbeth is very influential in the play. Would Macbeth have carried out the murders without her?
- At the start she seems a strong character. Later she is tormented by what they have done. Put the following sentences in order to describe what happens to Lady Macbeth:

  1 Lady Macbeth sleepwalks and tries to wash imaginary blood from her hands.

  2 She plans to murder King Duncan.

  3 Lady Macbeth dies.

  4 She helps to make the King's servants look guilty.

  5 She tries to explain Macbeth's strange behaviour at the banquet.

- Now match these quotations to the events described above.

  A I'll gild the faces of the grooms withal

  B Pray you, keep seat. The fit is momentary

  C What, will these hands ne'er be clean?

  D He that's coming must be provided for

  E The Queen, my lord, is dead

- At the end of the play she is described as a 'fiend-like queen'. Do you think this is a fair description of Lady Macbeth?

FOCUS ON BANQUO

Banquo bravely fights alongside Macbeth at the beginning of the play. He is also with Macbeth when they meet the witches for the first time. He is told that his descendants will be Kings yet he is not tempted to do evil like Macbeth.

Christopher Ravenscroft as Banquo, RSC, 1993

• Which of these statements below might explain Banquo's behaviour?

1 He's content with what he has.

2 He's loyal to King Duncan.

3 He doesn't believe in witches.

4 He has no scheming wife to persuade him.

5 He is a good man who would never do wrong.

• Can you think of any other reasons?

• What sort of person do you think Banquo is? Can you find evidence in the play to suggest that he is:

   loyal

   brave

   honest?

• Banquo provides a contrast to Macbeth. Put in order the events that happen to Banquo.

1 He meets the three witches.

2 He is seen as a ghost by Macbeth.

3 He is welcomed by King Duncan after winning the battle.

4 He is suspicious of Macbeth's actions.

5 He is murdered but his son Fleance escapes.

• Now match these quotations with the events above.

A I fear thou playd'st most foully for 't

B O, treachery! Fly, good Fleance, fly, fly, fly!

C What are these, so withered and so wild in their attire?

D Noble Banquo, let me enfold thee and hold thee to my heart

E Thy bones are marrowless, thy blood is cold

FOCUS ON MACDUFF

Macduff is suspicious. He is worried about the way Macbeth is ruling Scotland. He goes to England to ask for help. He returns with an army to fight Macbeth.

Peter Guiness as Macduff, RSC, 1986

- Put in order the following events that happen to Macduff.

1 He kills Macbeth and cuts off his head.

2 He tells Macbeth he was born by caesarean.

3 The witches warn Macbeth to watch out for him.

4 He discovers King Duncan murdered at Macbeth's castle.

5 He goes to England to ask for help.

6 He is told that his wife and children have been murdered while he was in England.

- Now match these quotations to the events above.

A Thither Macduff is gone to pray the holy King upon his aid

B Ring the alarum bell! Murder and treason

C Behold where stands th' usurper's cursed head

D Beware Macduff. Beware the Thane of Fife

E Macduff was from his mother's womb untimely ripped

F What, all my pretty chickens and their dam at one fell swoop?

Earlier you investigated the death of Duncan, King of Scotland.

• Imagine you could bring back to life all the characters in order to hold an official enquiry into the death of Duncan.

1 List all the characters who died in the play.

2 List all the characters who could be suspects.

3 List all the characters who could be called as a witness (remember that there would be plenty of servants around).

4 Don't forget to look back at the police statement from page 68. Don't forget the 'Focus on Sheets'.

5 Give each member of the class a character to prepare. What did they see or hear?

6 Appoint a judge, prosecution, defence and jury. What evidence is there to support your case?

• Role play the investigations.

• Write a report on your findings. You could write a TV news report on the enquiry which includes interviews with witnesses and suspects.

WHAT DID YOU LEARN?

In this unit you have looked carefully at the play *Macbeth*. You have followed the plot. You have understood how Macbeth's ambition destroyed him in the end. You have used role play to help you think about the characters and what happens to them. Watching the play will have helped you to see how it all fits together. Now ask yourself these questions:

1 What drives Macbeth to kill the King and keep on killing?

2 Do you think Macbeth is man or monster?

3 What is the most exciting part of the play?

4 Can you choose one word to say what the play is really about?

5 What was your best piece of work (written or oral) in this unit? What pleased you about it?

EXTENSION TASKS

As an extension to this unit, choose one of the following tasks.

1 Look at some theatre programmes. Design your own for *Macbeth*. Find out more about Shakespeare and the play. Put this information into your programme.

2 Write your own version of the story of *Macbeth*. Make sure you get the sequence of events right.

3 You have been asked to write a page on King Macbeth for a history book. How would you describe him? What information is important?

UNIT FOUR

The Language
Detective

The language we use changes to suit different situations.
In this unit you will develop your skills as:

SPEAKERS AND LISTENERS

by spotting differences in the way people speak in different
   situations
by judging the evidence of witnesses

READERS

by sorting out facts and opinions
by studying how language conveys opinions

WRITERS

by writing a memo
by replying to a letter
by putting a report in order

Now turn the page to become a language detective...

THE ACCIDENT

There's been an accident.
Lots of people saw it.
But they all have a different story.
It's a job for...

...THE LANGUAGE DETECTIVE! (That's you!)

COLLECTING EVIDENCE

This is what the first witness says:

I didn't see it all. I saw the car overtake the van. It was a red car. There were kids in the back of the car. It looked to me as if they were playing up. Perhaps the children distracted the driver. I think she was going faster than the speed limit! Next thing I heard was a woman shouting 'Come back Snoopy!'

I saw a dog rush out. There was a loud squealing of brakes and then a huge crash. I can't say I liked the attitude of the van driver. He looked as if he hadn't shaved in days and he was making rude gestures. The dog was dead, of course. I blame the woman in the car.

The witness has given you some interesting information, but how useful is it?

- On a copy of this page, underline the bits about the accident that she actually saw. These are facts, so you can be sure that these are true.

- Put a wavy line under the bits that are just her opinion. You can't be sure about these.

- What do you suspect may have happened?

- Can you prove it yet?

- What questions do you need to ask to find out the truth? You may want to speak to other witnesses.

Here is a sketch of the scene of the accident:

You go on to question other witnesses.

The vermilion car
came to a sudden halt.
She was exceeding the speed limit.

The van driver had
concussion, and one
of the children had a
fractured arm.

The witnesses have used some unusual words – better check them!

MASTERCLASS: HOW TO USE A DICTIONARY

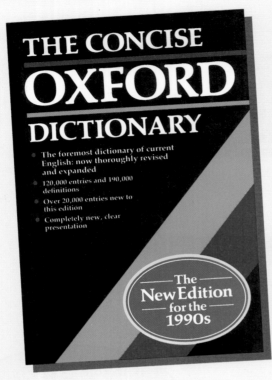

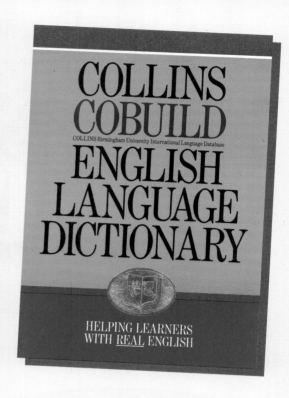

ALPHABETICAL ORDER

In a dictionary, the words are listed in **alphabetical order**.

The alphabet has 26 letters:

A B C D E F G H I J K L M N O P Q R S T U V W X Y Z

• Try to learn the order of the letters in the alphabet.

1 Look at the first five letters.

2 Cover them and say them.

3 Uncover them and check that you were right. When you know the first five, add five more letters and start again.

• See how much of the alphabet you can learn by the next lesson.

In your dictionary:

Age comes before Beauty
because A comes before B

Abacus comes before Alphabet
because AB comes before AL

After comes before Afternoon
because Afternoon has more letters

LOOKING THINGS UP

- Look up the unusual words used by the witnesses.

exceeding	vermilion
concussion	fractured

The middle of the dictionary is **m**.

Half way between the front and the middle is **e**.

Half way between the middle and the end is **r**.

Letter m

Letter r

Letter e

How long does it take you to look up the following words? Time yourself, or get someone to time you. Write down the time beside the word in your exercise book.

dictionary	detective	barometer	accent
dialect	formal	informal	

- Write down the meaning to prove you have found the word. Did you become any faster?

- Now write down the words in the order they come in the alphabet.

BACK ON THE BEAT...

That van driver weren't half narked. There's a dog nearby, dead cute. Did you see what happened to it?

The accident occurred on the High Street black-spot where similar accidents have occurred over the past year.

Police took two hours to clear away the wreckage from a crash in Parton High Street this morning, after a car smashed into an oncoming van.

A right slanging match were going on. Then they kind of swerved. Next thing you know the van's gone slap bang into the back of the car.

The first vehicle is a red family saloon, registration number J726 CFA.

Statements have been obtained from two witnesses and the drivers.

Pressure groups claim that there will be a serious accident if traffic lights aren't installed soon.

It all happened real quick, you know. I saw the car out of the corner of my eye. It looked like the kid were getting a telling off.

The vehicle is owned by the driver, Mrs J. Freehandle, of 15 Primrose Drive, Preston.

Occupants of both vehicles were said to be unharmed, but in a state of shock.

You have reports from three other people: a police officer, a reporter and a witness. Unfortunately, the notes get jumbled up.

- Look at the language used in each statement on page 90. Discuss with a partner: who said each statement?

- How did you work out who said what?

- What were the tell-tale clues? Discuss:

1 The words they chose

2 The tone they took

3 The way the sentences were constructed

WAYS OF USING LANGUAGE

When you speak to people at the accident, you hear the following ways of speaking:

jokes	surnames
swearing	insults
an exact description	opinions
guesses about what happened	gossip about the people involved
nick-names	place names

- Discuss which of these you can use in a formal report. Give reasons for all your choices.

- Make a list of five rules for writing a fair and useful accident report. Think about the type of report that a police officer might write.

MASTERCLASS: THE SPEAKING SCALE:
HOW WE SPEAK IN DIFFERENT SITUATIONS

It does not matter who we are or where we come from, we
all change the way we speak. These changes depend on
- who we are speaking to
- why we are speaking.

In some situations we feel relaxed. In others we may have
an important job to do. This will affect what we want to say
and the way we say it.

At one end of the speaking scale is formal talk which is
polite and careful to be clear.

At the other end of the speaking scale is informal talk such
as chat.

- Copy the speaking scale into your book.

- Some situations are more formal than others. Where do the following situations go on your speaking scale? Start with the most formal:

at the swimming pool	a family meal at a table
in a noisy playground	in a court of law
in the classroom	at the supermarket check-out till
in the headteacher's office	on the phone to a friend
a job interview	to your parents asking for money

- Now think about the different ways you would greet people. Make a list of different words you might use and put them on the scale.

- Now do this again with phrases to get someone's attention.

- Think about the way you change your language when you want to be formal. Complete these two sentences:

When I want to be formal, I use...

When I want to be informal, I use...

BACK ON THE BEAT...

- Complete the first part of your report keeping to the facts. Use these starters:

The accident took place on .... at .... between

a .... and a ....

The accident happened when...

The damage to the van consists of...

The damage to the car consists of...

The two vehicles are now...

I am planning to...

- Look at your 'detective' diary for today's work on page 95. Decide how formal you will have to be for each appointment. Use a scale of 1 to 10 (where 10 is the most formal).
  You can use a number more than once.

- Now have a go at writing your own diary. Try to include as many different speaking situations as you can during one day. Put each situation on a speaking scale of 1 to 10.

- For three different events in your diary, write down the different things you said and the way you said them. An example has been done for you:

> **10.50 Spoke to class** *(speaking scale 7)*
>
> *This was quite a formal situation, even though I knew everybody had to stand in front of the class in turn. I told them about my holiday, using some funny stories.*

- Look again at your 'detective' diary.
  In pairs, discuss and write down the things you would say in three of the situations. Be prepared to report them back to the class.

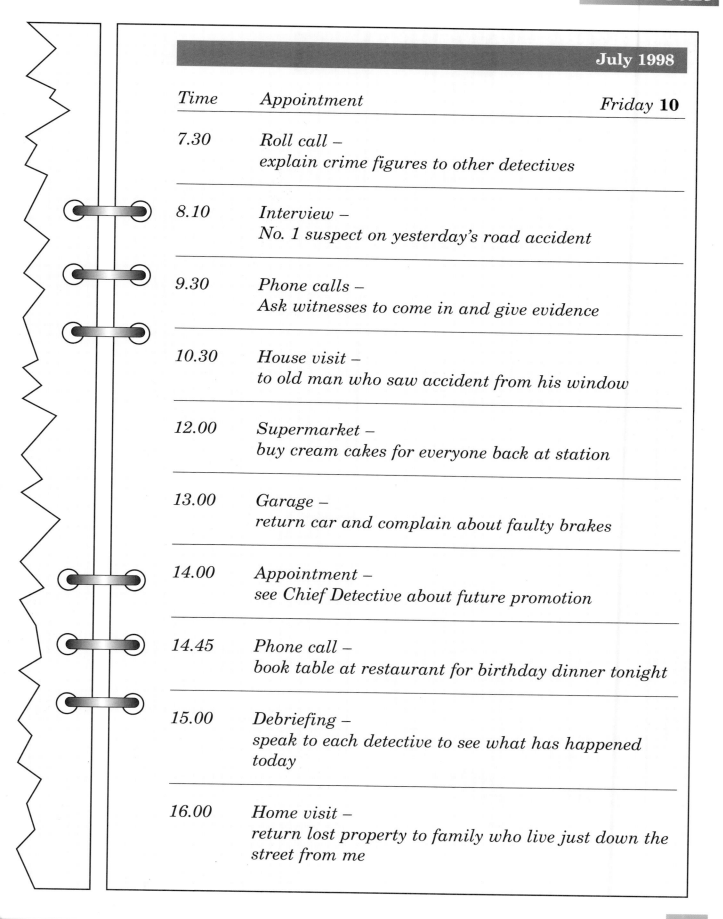

July 1998

Time	Appointment	Friday **10**
7.30	Roll call – explain crime figures to other detectives	
8.10	Interview – No. 1 suspect on yesterday's road accident	
9.30	Phone calls – Ask witnesses to come in and give evidence	
10.30	House visit – to old man who saw accident from his window	
12.00	Supermarket – buy cream cakes for everyone back at station	
13.00	Garage – return car and complain about faulty brakes	
14.00	Appointment – see Chief Detective about future promotion	
14.45	Phone call – book table at restaurant for birthday dinner tonight	
15.00	Debriefing – speak to each detective to see what has happened today	
16.00	Home visit – return lost property to family who live just down the street from me	

MAKING A STATEMENT

There is a difference between the way we speak and the way we write.

After the accident you interview the lady with the dog. This is what she says:

It must have been about 8.30.
I was chatting to Edna just by the zebra crossing.
Well, all I know is that Snoopy – he's my dog – was standing
right there one minute then next thing I know I hear this almighty
crash – and I look up and there's the van ploughing into the back of the
car. There was glass everywhere. The dog – well he was lying there, in the
road – I could see he was dead at once. I loved that dog – I really did. The
trouble is – the traffic on this road, it just speeds by – they don't give a
damn about us residents – they don't look where they're going, do
they Edna? Well, they were alright – the drivers I mean – all
they could do was shout at each other and all I could think
of was poor Snoopy – how will I tell my Fred?

You need a formal statement from this witness, saying exactly what she saw.

- What exactly **did** she see? Help her to write a report starting like this:

  I was standing by the zebra crossing in the High Street talking to my friend Mrs Edna Norris when I noticed that my dog Snoopy had slipped away. I did not see how the accident was caused, but I did see…

- How is the written report different from the spoken report?

- What was wrong with simply copying down her spoken words?

- Finish the statement.

MASTERCLASS: WHAT DO YOU CALL YOURS?

The following are all local words for 'nose':

conk snout honker cheese cutter beak

Some people think 'conk' means 'nose' because it comes from 'conch', which is a spiral-shaped shell.

- Look again at the other local words for nose. Why do you think they are used? Draw pictures to help you explain.

The nose is a very important part of our life. We use it in many everyday sayings.

PAY THROUGH THE NOSE!

This saying comes from a tax in Ireland in the 19th century. If you did not pay, your nose was cut open!

- Can you guess either the saying or what it means using the clues below?

Falling quickly	➡	NOSE _____
?	⬅	NOSE TO THE GRINDSTONE
A curious person	➡	NOSY _____
Someone who annoys you	➡	___ ___ ___ NOSE
?	⬅	TURN UP YOUR NOSE

MASTERCLASS (CONTINUED): TAKING THE WORDS OUT OF YOUR MOUTH

The following words are used in different parts of the country.

Do you recognise any of these words?

lairy   mouthy   out of order   cocky

All of these are local words for someone who is being cheeky or rude.

CREATE YOUR OWN LOCAL WORD DICTIONARY

- Start by thinking of as many local words as you can for the following:

money	women
parts of the body	wonderful
children	not interesting
men	horrible

- Now add other words of your own to the list.

RHYMING SLANG

Cockneys are people who live in the East End of London. They have their own local speech, or dialect.

Cockney rhyming slang is a way of speaking that can only be understood by locals. The police cannot always understand their speech!

When a Cockney says: 'I was so tired, I went straight up the apple and pears to my Uncle Ned!'
he means: 'I was so tired I went up the stairs to my bed!'

- Match these slang words with their meanings:

Plates of meat	eyes
France and Spain	wife
Trouble and strife	trousers
Round the houses	rain
Mince pies	feet

- Pick two words. Explain why the Cockneys chose those rhymes.
- Make up your own rhyming slang. Follow this example:

  Nose rhymes with **hose** – add **garden** = **garden hose**

- Write a secret message to your friend in your own rhyming slang.

BACK ON THE BEAT: MORE WITNESSES

It is time to question two more witnesses to the accident: Mrs Godwin is a nervous old lady who is upset. Mr Black is a man with very strong options, and he is cross.

You can tell a lot about these witnesses from the way they act.
You can tell a lot from their **body language**.

- Think of a television with no sound. List what you can tell about people's thoughts and feelings by just looking. You could start with the expressions on the faces.

BODY LANGUAGE

Look at the people in the drawings below.

- In pairs, discuss what you think their body language shows.

- In pairs, mime the interviews between the language
detective and the two witnesses on page 99. Use body
language to show what they are saying.

MASTERCLASS: HOW TO SPOT CLUES IN HOW PEOPLE SPEAK

Like body language, you can use words to show how you feel:

'That is a **disgusting** habit!'

Disgusting is the describing word (an adjective). It shows us what the person feels about the habit.

Every adjective has a different strength, so you must choose one that fits the situation.

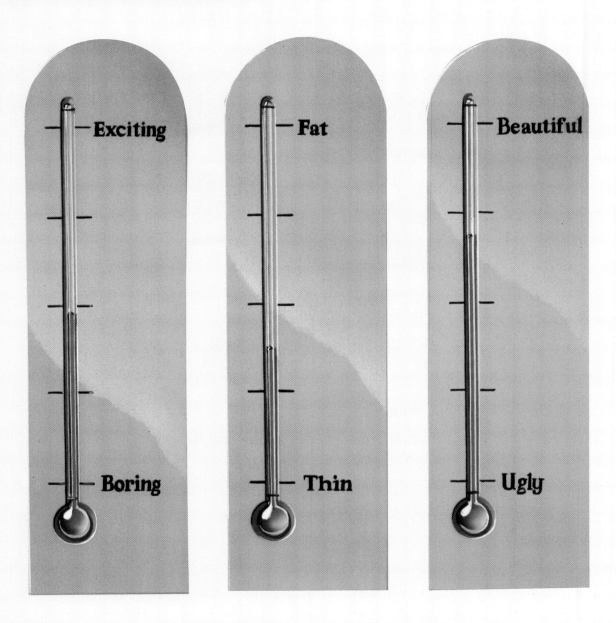

MASTERCLASS (CONTINUED):

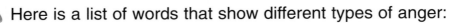

Here is a list of words that show different types of anger:

upset   livid   disappointed   annoyed   irritated   cross   furious

• Copy a thermometer like the one on page 101.
  Put the words in order on the thermometer, from most
  to least angry. Look up the ones you don't know in a
  dictionary.

• Four people have read the same book. Can you decide
  who liked it the most?

Discuss the order with the rest of the class.

• In groups or on your own, make your own language
  thermometers, using one of the following words to start
  you off:

loud   hard   small   sad

Hint: think of an object such as a person, a painting, a
party or a lesson to describe in different ways.

BACK ON THE BEAT: INTERVIEWING THE DRIVERS

It's time to interview the drivers.

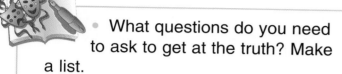

- What questions do you need to ask to get at the truth? Make a list.
- How will you treat the drivers?

- What tone will you use?
- In pairs, one be the detective and the other be the van driver or Janet Freehandle. Read the notes below then act out the interview.

John Blackwell:

Van Driver   Local printing company

25, single

It was an important delivery. He is angry because the crash made him late.

He thinks the interview is a waste of time.

You suspect that he was driving too fast.

Janet Freehandle:

Solicitor   Large law firm

43, married with children

She was taking her children to school. She is upset and still in shock.

You think that she was not paying attention to her driving.

- Now swap roles. The other person can be the detective this time.
- Write up one of the interviews as a script. Look at the next page for some tips.

MASTERCLASS: SCRIPT WRITING

A script only records who speaks and what is said.
Look at how this script is written.

Detective: What speed were you travelling at?

Woman: I don't recall.

Detective: I find that hard to believe!

- How can you tell who is speaking?
- Which part do you say aloud?
- Why do you need a capital letter when the speaking starts?
- How many different ways has a sentence ended?

BACK ON THE BEAT...

Next day, you receive the letter on page 105.

Should you give in? Will you give in?

- Write a reply to Mr Grunter's letter.
  Try to be firm, but tactful and polite.
  Follow these steps:

1 Use a photocopy of the letter on page 106. Cut out all the pieces.

2 Choose the parts of the letter you want to use.

3 Organise a reply on a sheet of A4 paper. At least Mr Grunter knows how to present a good letter, so you can copy his layout.

Inglewood House
Linton Road
Patwood
Surrey
RH2 4US

Language Detective
Language Unit
Green Street
Ashton
Surrey
GU4 7JH

17th July 1998

Dear Language Detective,

I do appreciate that detectives have a difficult job. There are more and more crimes against language and they must be stamped out.

Yesterday I heard from my daughter Mrs Freehandle that she had been interviewed about an accident in her car. I was shocked and rather sad to hear this.

You must understand how embarrassing it could be for a man in my position to have an investigation into members of my family. I am anxious that the police do not over-react to what was, after all, a minor accident.

I am sure that my good friend and your boss, the Chief Inspector will agree with me that this case should be dropped.

Yours sincerely,

Peter Grunter

P. Grunter

Inglewood House	Mr P. Grunter
Surrey	Linton Road
GU4 7JH	Patwood
RH2 4US	18th July 1998
Dear Mr Grunter,	Language Unit
Green Street	Ashton
Surrey	Yours sincerely,

Keep your nose out of this investigation. It's none of your business!

Life is hard sometimes, but don't be upset. It will blow over.
One day you will look back on this and smile.

Thank you for your letter. I understand your concern but the law
applies to everyone.

What difference does it make if she's your daughter?

No one will notice.

I am sorry. I did not realise Mrs Freehandle was your daughter.
The investigation will be dropped at once.

I am sorry for any embarrassment this may have caused.

You have no right to ask me to drop the investigation.

You have a nerve!

The investigation is going ahead and we will write to Mrs Freehandle in
the next few days to explain what will happen next.

Looking back, I can see that Mrs Freehandle was justified in killing the dog.

I was delighted to hear of your interest in the Freehandle case.

Do let me know if there are any other favours I can do for you.

WRITING A MEMO

You also receive this memo from your boss:

memo

To: Language Detective

From: Chief Inspector

Re: Grunter case

There are a number of messages from Mr Grunter on my answerphone about a case you are on. What's the problem? What actions are you taking?

 • Write a memo in reply. On a copy of this page, fill in the top part of the memo, then start with the line given.

memo

To:

From:

Re:

For your information, I attach the letter I have…

THE TRUTH AT LAST!

This is what really happened:

NEWSFLASH

- Present a radio news bulletin about the accident. You can make up your own story about the accident, or use one of these ideas.

SNOOPY SNUFFS IT

TV dog killed in road accident

GRUNTER JAILED

Foiled attempt to pervert justice

TRAFFIC CHAOS

Town at standstill following crash

MASTERCLASS: SPOTTING CLUES IN THE WAY WE SPEAK

As a Language Detective, you can find clues about people's background in the way they speak.

The way a person uses language is often affected by the part of the country they come from.

ACCENT

Accent is the way a person says a word. For example, the word 'bath' can be said in two main ways:

1 The 'a' sounds like the 'a' in cat

2 The 'a' sounds like 'ar'

DIALECT

Dialect is a local way of expressing things.

- What local words do you know for:

  plimsolls?

  playtime?

- What local expressions do you know for:

  something annoying?

  being drunk?

- Do you know any ways of speaking from other parts of the country?

MASTERCLASS (CONTINUED):

• Read the passage below, where a woman is speaking about servants. What do you notice about the language used?

• Find some examples of:

1 accent (how she pronounces words)

2 dialect and local words (how she expresses herself).

• Set your examples out as shown below.
Two examples have been done for you.

Accent	Explanation
Ha'n't = had not	*The ' shows that the letters 'd' and 'o' have been left out. The word sounds different.*

Dialect	Explanation
It were nothing = *It was nothing*	*A plural is used instead of a singular verb. 'Were' can only be used for more than one person, e.g. 'we were'.*

It were nothing for a girl to be sent away to service when she were eleven years old. This meant leaving the family as she had never been parted from for a day in her life before, and going to some place miles away to be treated like something as ha'n't got as much sense or feeling as a dog. I've got nothing against girls going into good service.

In my opinion, good service in a properly run big house were a wonderful thing for a lot o' girls who never would ha' seen anything different all the days o' their lives if they ha'n't gone. It were better than working on the land, then, and if it still existed now, I reckon I'd rather see any o' my daughters to be a good housemaid or a well trained parlour-maid than a dolled-up shop assistant or a factory worker.

From *The Fenland Chronicle* by Sybil Marshall

Now read this passage:

These farmers were a jumped up, proud lot who di'n't know how to treat the people who worked for 'em. They took advantage o' the poor peoples' need to get their girls off their hands to get little slaves for nearly nothing. The conditions were terrible. One little girl I know'd went when she were eleven to a great lonely farmhouse on the highlands, miles from anywhere. The very next day after she got there, the grandmother o' the household died and were laid out on the bed straight away.

Then the heartless woman of the house sent poor little Eva to scrub the floor o' the room where the corpse laid. She were frit to death, an' no wonder, but she 'as to do it. When she were cleaning under the bed, the corpse suddenly rumbled and groaned as the wind passed out of it, and to Eva's dying day she never forgot the terror o' that moment. I can't think there were many folks as 'ould 'ave bin as cruel as that, but when I remember the general conditions o' such poor mites, it makes me think again.

From *'The Fenland Chronicle'* by Sybil Marshall.

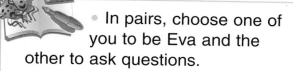

- In pairs, choose one of you to be Eva and the other to ask questions.

- If you are Eva:

  tell the story of what happened when you were asked to clean under the dead body.

- If you are asking the questions:

  – think about what you want to know about Eve's experiences

  – write down three questions to ask Eva.

WHAT DID YOU LEARN?

How much have you learnt from being a language detective?
Answer the questions below.

1   Can you say the letters of the alphabet in order?

2   What letter comes in the middle of an English dictionary?

3   What is the difference between formal and informal speech?

4   Suggest some rules for writing a formal report.

5   Name three things that make people change the way they speak.

6   Give two examples of groups of describing words that express the same idea. List them in order of strength.

7   What is body language? Give two examples.

8   What is the difference between accent and dialect?

9   What kinds of questions are useful in interviews?

10 Draw a diagram to show how to lay out a letter.

HOW DID YOU DO?

1   Which part of this unit did you most enjoy? Can you explain what you liked about it?

2   In what ways is this work better than work you have done before?

3   If you had to go back to one section and do it again, which one would you choose and what would you do differently?

4   What do you think is the most important thing you have learned from being a language investigator?

UNIT FIVE

Scandal

In this unit you will learn how to be persuasive, and how to present a point of view.

You will develop your skills as:

SPEAKERS AND LISTENERS

by discussing some difficult decisions

by planning and presenting a speech

READERS

by sorting out facts and opinions

by studying how language conveys opinions

WRITERS

by filling out a form

by making notes towards a speech

by writing an article

Now turn the page to find out why Chris and Raheela have a problem...

IT'S A GREAT DAY FOR REDWOOD SCHOOL

IN TWO MINDS...

Chris and Raheela have a problem. They want to accuse
David Watson of pollution. If they do he won't want to give
their school any computers.

Which is more important:

• to have a computer for everyone in the school?

• to have a clean river?

• Look at the pictures above. Write down as many
  points as you can for

a) having a computer for everyone in the school

b) having a clean river.

GETTING YOUR MESSAGE ACROSS

Look at these two speeches:

A   Ladies and gentlemen, if the school has more computers we'll get better results and better jobs.

B   Can you imagine what a marvellous thing it will be for Redwood School, ladies and gentlemen, if every child in every class can have the use of their own computer? What happens at the moment?

In every IT lesson we have to cram four pupils round one computer. As a result, three out of four students are bored. With one computer to one student everyone will be learning at a much faster rate. Our exam results are bound to improve.

- Which speech makes the point best? Why?
- Work in groups to plan two speeches:

Speech 1

➡ Start planning the speech for a cleaner river like this:
- *Ladies and gentlemen, think of all the advantages of a clean river.*
- *Think of the anglers, who fish in the river…*

➡ Think of two or three points to make about anglers, for example:
- *fish will thrive in clean water*
- *clean riverbank*
- *will encourage more anglers*

➡ Think of two or three points to make about the view.
- *And what about people who just like a beautiful view…*

➡ Think of two or three points to make about children.
- *Then there are children who like to paddle or swim…*

Speech 2

➡ Make up some sentence starters for Speech 2 in favour of more computers in school.

➡ Under each sentence starter, think of two or three points to make.

- Choose which speech to make, and rehearse it.

- When all the groups have made their speeches, the class can vote on the best speech.

- In groups, discuss what makes a good speech.

DOES THE STORY STAND UP?

Chris and Raheela get their chance to
talk to the boss. But before they go in
they think hard:
What do they know that is **fact** –
something they **know** to be true?
What, on the other hand, is **opinion** –
something that **might** be true?

- Look at the statements below.
- Discuss each statement in pairs. Decide whether
each statement is fact or opinion.
- On a copy of this grid, tick the correct column.

Statement	Fact	Opinion
There are dead fish in the river.		
The pollution comes from the factory.		
Pollution is killing the fish.		
Stopping pollution is less important than a drug for old people.		
Stopping pollution is more important than a drug for old people.		
There have been cases of tummy upset.		
Clean water is more important than computers for the school.		

Chris and Raheela put their point of view to the radio station's boss and Mike, the legal expert.

- • Split into groups of four. Choose who will take the parts of Raheela, Chris, the Radio Station Boss and Mike.

- • Act out the discussion. Raheela and Chris must persuade Mike and the Radio Station Boss to report the story.

HELP

Remember that it is important to be tactful. Put your point of view firmly, but don't spoil a good point by being rude or aggressive.

THE NEXT DAY

I'LL TELL YOU WHAT WE'LL DO. WE'LL PUT AN ARTICLE IN THE SCHOOL MAGAZINE!

GREAT IDEA! BUT WE'D BETTER NOT GO OVER TOP.

I'LL TELL YOU WHAT. WE'LL BOTH WRITE ARTICLES, THEN WE'LL SEE WHICH ONE IS THE BEST.

HOW FAR CAN WE GO?

Chris and Raheela both write articles. Chris blames David Watson's factory for the pollution. Raheela is more careful. She describes the pollution as a mystery. She doesn't jump to any conclusions.

Extracts from the two articles are given on the opposite page. Can you tell who wrote each line?

- Using a photocopy of page 123, cut up the boxes.
- Put the lines under the right headline and in the right order.
- You do not have the parts of the articles which tell you about the factory owned by David Watson.

  1 What do you think Raheela's article would say about the factory?

  2 What would Chris's article say?

- Write an extra paragraph for each article, which fits in with the approach of the rest.

by Raheela Khan

Ten-year-old Darren Atkins was another sufferer, after taking a two-minute paddle.

A large number of dead fish have been found in the river. What has happened? It is a mystery.

Tests on river water prove that aluminium sulphate is the killer.

WATSON FACTORY POLLUTING RIVER

Other strange things have happened in the past few weeks.

Thousands of fish are dying in the river. They have been killed by poison. The poison is a chemical called aluminium sulphate.

We have heard that some people have had upset stomachs. They all live along the river.

MYSTERY OF DEAD FISH

An outbreak of upset stomachs is almost certainly linked to aluminium sulphate.

by Chris Bloom

Samples of the river water have been tested. They show very high levels of aluminium sulphate.

A ten-year-old boy, Darren Atkins, also came out in a rash after paddling in the river.

Several other incidents of pollution have been reported.

THE EYE IN THE SKY

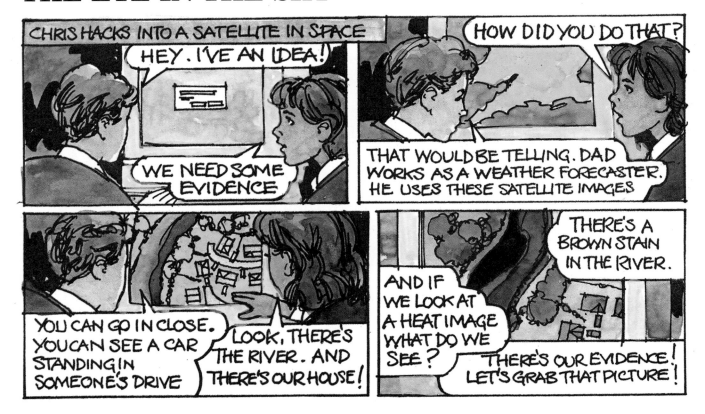

Chris and Raheela have hacked into a weather satellite. Out in space there are thousands of satellites. Some transmit TV signals. Some monitor weather patterns. Some are used to watch troop movements during wartime.

• Do you think Chris and Raheela were right to hack into a private computer system?

SECURITY OR INTRUSION?

There are many other ways in which our movements are watched.

- Can you think of other places where the public are filmed?

- What are the advantages of spy cameras?

- What are the disadvantages?

- How would you feel if a closed circuit television camera was installed in every classroom? What if the film was shown to parents?

PANIC STATIONS

PEOPLE GET TO HEAR OF THE ARTICLE IN THE SCHOOL MAGAZINE. SUDDENLY PEOPLE COME FORWARD WITH MORE SYMPTOMS.

WATER RUNS ORANGE

'I JUST HAD A SHOWER AND THIS HAPPENED...'

I CAN'T EVEN REMEMBER IF I CAME BY CAR, OR ON THE TRAIN...

CAR PARK

OTHERS GET SEVERE STOMACH PAINS

SUDDENLY THERE IS FEAR IN THE AREA

DO NOT APPROACH

DANGER

CROWDS GATHER AT THE GATES OF THE FACTORY

CLAIRE'S DIARY

Claire, alone in her room, keeps a diary in which she records her thoughts. Whose side should she be on?

It is very difficult for Claire to make up her mind. She knows that the factory employs hundreds of people in the town. They would lose their jobs if the factory closed.

She knows that her father has worked hard all his life for the business. He is a kind man at heart and he cares about the town and its people. She knows that the factory makes pills to reduce the pain of rheumatism.

But she also knows that her father has failed to clean up the water because it would cost too much. She knows the problems the pollution has caused.

Here are two extracts from Claire's diary:

MAY

Monday 11th

Another argument is going on. I'm in my bedroom but I can't help hearing. Mum's on at Dad again. They are talking about the purification plant. Dad says he can't afford it. I think she's right…

MAY

Tuesday 12th

Today Dad had a letter from an old lady. She told him how much his drug had helped her rheumatism. Suddenly I can't help seeing things differently…

- Now go on and finish this diary entry. Include all the reasons why Claire thinks her mother is right.

- Now go on and finish this diary entry. Include all the reasons why Claire now thinks her father could be right.

THE APPLICATION

APPLYING FOR A GRANT

• Fill in the form below, as if you were David Watson.

EUROPEAN COMMISSION FOR THE ENVIRONMENT

Application for Grant

Name of applicant:

Name of business:

Type of business:

Nature of pollution (name the chemicals if possible):

Explain the damage caused by the pollution:

1   To fish or animals…

2   To people …

What would the grant be used for?

Give the two most important reasons why you feel the grant should be given to you.

1

2

WHAT WOULD YOU DO?

Chris, Raheela and other characters in the story are faced with many difficult decisions. They are not alone! Life is full of difficult decisions.

- Six situations are described on the following pages. In each one a difficult decision must be made.
- In groups, read about each situation in turn and discuss:
  - what you **should** do
  - what you **would** do.

CAN IT BE RIGHT TO STEAL?

John Brown's wife is suffering from cancer. John hears about a wonderful new drug. It is made by a big drug company. It has taken the company 20 years to develop the drug. It has cost them millions of pounds to make.

The price of the drug is £5000. John does not have the money. He borrows £2000 and offers it to the company. He says his wife will die if they do not help.

The company refuses. They say that if they sold the drug cheaply to Mr Brown, then other people would want the same. If they did not charge the full price they would lose money.

That night John breaks into the company's offices. He steals the new drug and gives it to his wife.

Was he right?

CAN YOU TAKE THE OFFER?

You are the Chairman of a Formula One car racing team. Your wife was a very heavy smoker. A year ago she died of lung cancer.

Your team has been sponsored by a soft drinks company. Last year your team lost many races, and the sponsor pulled out. The team is in a very difficult position. It was about to buy a new star driver. Now the team cannot afford him. At the last moment a new company offers to sponsor the team. But there is one problem. It is a tobacco company.

You are in two minds. Your team really needs the new deal. But your wife died from smoking. Do you accept the offer?

WOULD YOU GO ON TELEVISION?

You work for a company that sells burglar alarms. Many of your customers are old people. You know that many sales staff get old people to buy alarms by frightening them with stories of break-ins and muggings.

You are invited to appear on a programme which tells the truth about these sales. If you go on the programme and tell the truth, your friends at work will feel you are letting them down. You might also lose your job.

On the other hand, you feel that it is wrong to frighten old people into buying alarms. Do you agree to go on the programme?

DO YOU KEEP THE MONEY?

Your money has been taken by the school bully. Walking home you see something lying on the pavement. It is a wallet. Inside there is a pension book with a name and address on it. There is also £50.

You want to keep the money to buy a new computer game. At the same time, you recognise the name and address on the pension book. It is the grumpy old man who lives round the corner. Do you keep the money?

WOULD YOU TAKE THE COMPUTER AND RUN?

You go to a big store and buy a computer. You pay with a cheque. The assistant is very busy and makes a mistake. Instead of taking the cheque and giving you a receipt, he gives you your own cheque back and puts the receipt in the till.

Do you keep your cheque – or do you go back in and pay?

HOW CAN YOU HELP?

You go to a new school and are worried about being bullied. A tough girl called Kelly becomes your friend and looks after you.

Then another new girl called Sharon arrives in the class. Kelly starts to bully Sharon. Sharon comes to ask your advice. Should she report Kelly for bullying? You hate to see Sharon being bullied. But Kelly is your best friend because she looked after you when you were new. What advice do you give Sharon?

WORDS THAT BITE

When people hold strong opinions they use strong language to put them over.

   Language that 'carries an opinion' in this way is called **loaded language.**

short

stumpy

tall

tiny

lanky

petite

small

lofty

big

pintsize

- If you liked Matthew, which words would you choose from the word pool? Why?

- If you liked Luke, which words would you choose from the word pool? Why?

- Is it ever right to use the other words? When? Why?

BEFORE AND AFTER STORIES

Now read these articles about pollution on the River Mawson.
One was written before a clean up. The other article was
written after the clean up.

BEFORE

What is the cause of pollution in the River Mawson? The finger has been pointed at paper mills. Outside Dutton Paper Mills, two pipes have been spewing out filth into the river.

Harry Bolton is a Water Inspector. He was quick to condemn the factory. 'It's disgusting. All my tests show levels of pollution that are far too high. Isn't it time some of these factory owners started putting the environment before profits?'

Jenny Barnes lives by the river. She agreed. 'I've stood by the pipes and seen the oily black gunge they pump out. No wonder wildlife and vegetation are being destroyed.'

AFTER

For the first time in many years salmon have been found swimming in the River Mawson. Anglers can spot the fish easily in the sparkling, clear water.

'It's brilliant that the river has been cleaned up,' said Jenny Barnes, who lives nearby. 'It's lovely to see the river back to its real self. It's a really pretty view now, when I look out of my window.'

Water Inspector Harry Bolton spoke warmly of the efforts made by the paper mills. 'They really cleaned up their act. Salmon are the sign of a healthy river, because it means they can breathe in the water.'

- Make two word pools. Call the first pool 'Before'. Call the second pool 'After'.

- In the 'Before' pool write all the examples of loaded language that make you feel that the river is badly polluted.

- In the 'After' pool write all the words that make you feel that the river is now clean and pleasant.

WHAT DID YOU LEARN?

In this unit you have had to make some difficult decisions. You have learned how to be persuasive and how to form an opinion. Can you:

1 Explain how you should go about planning a speech?

2 Name three things you can do to make a good speech?

3 Explain the difference between a fact and an opinion?

4 Explain how the same story can be reported differently?

5 Name three things that help to make a discussion go well?

6 Name three things you should bear in mind in making difficult decisions?

7 Explain what loaded language is, using an example?

HOW DID YOU DO?

1 Which part of this unit did you most enjoy? Can you explain what you liked about it?

2 In what ways is this work better than work you have done before?

3 If you had to go back to one section and do it again, which one would you choose and what would you do differently?

4 Will you look at arguments differently now? In what ways?

Stone Cold

Stone Cold is a novel about homelessness by Robert Swindells. In this unit you will develop your skills as:

SPEAKERS AND LISTENERS

by discussing key issues in the novel
by acting out role plays
by making tape-recordings

READERS

by reading and thinking about parts of the novel
by reading biographical and background information

WRITERS

by making jottings and notes in a reading log
by writing in a wide variety of forms

Turn the page to meet the author of *Stone Cold*…

ROBERT SWINDELLS – A BIOGRAPHY

Robert Swindells was born in Bradford in 1939. He was the eldest of five children. He left school at 15 and worked on a local newspaper until he was 17, when he joined the RAF. He served for three years in the UK and Germany. After leaving the RAF he had a variety of jobs in factories and offices. Between 1967 and 1969 he took five GCE O-levels at night school. He went to college in 1969 to train as a teacher. While he was at college he wrote a children's novel. It was published in 1973. He worked as a teacher from 1972 to 1980. He wrote in his spare time, and then became a full-time author.

He was an active member of the anti-nuclear movement and he took a master's degree in Peace Studies at the University of Bradford. In 1987 he was jailed for seven days for his part in a CND 'Snowball' non-violent action. Robert has written more than 50 books for young people. He has won a number of awards, including the Carnegie Medal. He is married. He has two grown-up daughters and three grandchildren. He lives on the Yorkshire moors.

WHY I WROTE THE NOVEL

Why did Robert Swindells choose to write a novel on homelessness?
Read the author's own answer to this question.

As an infrequent visitor to London (three, four times a year) it was particularly noticeable to me how the numbers of homeless youngsters in the capital had been growing throughout the eighties. I had it in the back of my mind to write a novel on the subject, and when the then Housing Minister, Sir George Young, made his infamous remark that the homeless are the sort of people one steps on when coming out of the opera, I felt indignant enough to begin.

I wrote to the charities Alone in London and Centrepoint Soho telling them of my intention and requesting information. Both were most helpful, sending packs of material which proved invaluable. However, it dawned on me eventually that if I was to write convincingly about life on the street, I was going to have to experience it at first hand.

Accordingly in the spring of 1992 I let my hair grow long, refrained from bathing for a week or two and took myself off to London and to Camden High Street, dressed in my oldest clothes and dangling a bedroll. I spent three consecutive nights in the area around the tube station, Pratt Street (where one of my publishers had their offices) and the Lock Market. I was able to strike up conversations with a number of homeless youngsters, who thought I'd come from Bradford looking for work. One night at one a.m. a man approached the doorway I was sitting in, deposited a bagful of hot Chinese food at my side and hurried off without a word. Another night I was hugged by a hulking Scots alcoholic whom I'd thought was about to murder me. Three nights – three warm spring nights were enough for me, and I was over fifty. What it must feel like at sixteen I shudder to imagine.

I ought to emphasise here that I don't claim, on the strength of those three nights, to have experienced homelessness.

A publisher friend had kindly made his lovely flat available to me so that I could sleep in the daytime, and I could have fled there at night too if I'd needed to. I was able to find out for myself what it feels like to lie on concrete for hours on end, to observe what goes on on Camden High Street at three in the morning, and learn at second hand about some of the dangers homeless youngsters face every night of their lives. This proved to be priceless when I was writing the book, but I don't delude myself but that if I had to do it for real I'd be dead in a month.

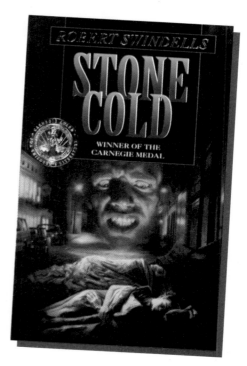

- Discuss in groups all the things you expect this novel to be about. What events might happen in it? Take your ideas from what the author says about the background to the story, and the book cover.

- Imagine that *you* are planning a story. It is based on homeless young people living on the streets of London. What ideas would you have for the **plot** (what happens in the story)?

CALL THAT A HOME?

- If you had the choice, which of these homes would you live in?
- Make a list of your top ten requirements in a home. You might include: heat, shelter, love, TV...

LONELY?

LOST?

AFRAID?

DIRTY?

SCROUNGERS?

COLD?

• Imagine meeting these two people sleeping rough in the street. Discuss with a partner the thoughts and feelings you would have about them. Report back to the whole class.

LINK'S STORY

Now read the first page of the novel.

You can call me Link. It's not my name, but it's what I say when anybody asks, which isn't often. I'm invisible, see. One of the invisible people. Right now I'm sitting in a doorway watching the passers-by. They avoid looking at me. They're afraid I want something they've got, and they're right. Also, they don't want to think about me. They don't like reminding I exist. Me, and those like me. We're living proof that everything's not all right and we make the place untidy.

Hang about and I'll tell you the story of my fascinating life.

   • Think carefully about this opening page. Discuss these questions:

1 Why has Link changed his name?

2 Who are the 'invisible people'?

3 Why are passers-by afraid of him?

4 What makes him say 'We're living proof that everything's not all right…'?

5 Why is Link sitting in a doorway?

   • Now write some questions of your own. What do you want to find out as you read on?

STARTING YOUR OWN READING LOG

WHAT IS A READING LOG?

A reading log is a book in which you write down all your thoughts, ideas and questions about the novel you are reading.

PROMPTS FOR WRITING

You can write anything you like in your log, but you might consider:

1 Setting – where and when the story takes place

2 Characters – the people in the story

3 Plot – what happens in the story

4 Language – how the story is written

5 Themes – ideas and messages you get from the story

6 Wide reading – how this story compares to others you have read.

You could start your log with the questions you've already thought of, after reading the first page of the novel.

This is how one student began her log:

Monday 5/8/98

'Stone Cold'

I've just started 'Stone Cold'. Page 1 is a bit puzzling. Why has Link changed his name? Doesn't he like his real name? I think he might want to forget his old life. Maybe he's one of the people on the front cover. Maybe he's homeless, sleeping rough on the streets.

When I see beggars in Bristol I get a bit frightened. I normally rush past them in a hurry. They're dirty and often drunk. I'd hate to be like them. I reckon this is a story about being homeless…

• Now start your own reading log. Remember you can choose any part of the novel to write about. Look out for these reminders as you work on the unit.

LAST CHRISTMAS AT HOME...

Now look carefully at this section of the novel.

Christmas didn't help. I spent it at Carole's which was kind of her and Chris, but it was still the worst Christmas I'd ever had. For a start, there was my present. Carole and Mum had put their money together and got me this sleeping-bag. A really posh job. Quilted, waterproof, the lot. It must have cost a bomb and I knew they only meant to be kind, but it said something to me. It said they thought of me as a dosser – as someone who might always be a dosser, so he might as well be as comfy as possible. It hurt like hell, but I didn't let them see. And I've got to admit it's come in handy ever since.

   Anyway, there was that, and then there was Boxing Day. Boxing Day Mum came round, and she brought Vince with her. I can only think that Carole had never told Chris the full story about him, or surely Chris wouldn't have had him in the house. Anyway, they came for dinner and stayed till one o'clock next morning, and of course everybody got drunk. Everybody except me. And once he got a skinful, Vince started making cracks about me. Don't ask me why. I was a disgrace, he said, stuffing myself with my sister's grub. Sitting there with my long hair and tatty clothes, making Mum feel guilty when she'd had nothing to feel guilty about. I was a scrounger, a sponger and a layabout, and I ought to be looking for work instead of sitting with a face as long as a fiddle, spoiling everybody's Christmas.

   It didn't feel like peace on earth, I can tell you that. There wasn't a lot of goodwill toward men floating about. And the worst thing was, nobody stuck up for me. Not even my sister. It was then I knew I'd worn out my welcome, even here. So.

Here is an extract from the BBC TV script of the Christmas Day scene:

Carole: Come on, let's open your present.

(She picks up a huge parcel from under the Christmas tree)

It's from me and Mum.

Vince: There's some of my money in there, and all.

Carole: And Vince.

(She holds out the present)

Go on.

Vince: Oh, he'll take it, he's good at that.

Lesley: Stop it, Vince.

(Link opens his present – it's an expensive looking sleeping bag. He looks around their faces – all smiling)

Link: It's brilliant, thanks.

• Work in a group of five. Each of you take the part of one of the characters:

Link
Lesley (his mum)
Carole (his sister)
Vince (his step-father)
Chris (his brother-in-law)

• Think about Boxing Day. Act out what happens at the meal table. Use the account on p146 to help you.

• You could plan and write your play in the same way that the BBC **dramatised** the Christmas Day scene.

If you **dramatise** something, you take an existing story and turn it into a play. This happens a lot on TV. Can you think of any other dramatisations you have seen on TV?

WHO'S WHO?

Can you work out who's who?

- Ask your teacher for a photocopy of these pages, then cut out each picture and paste it in your log.

- Write a short description for each character.

- Study one character in detail and think of questions for all the others.

- As a class, or in a group of four, take it in turns to put each character in the 'hot seat' (see the Help Box opposite). Ask each character questions. Try to find out what kind of person each is:
  1 What do they think?
  2 What do they want?
  3 What are they planning to do?

HOT-SEATING

You can hot-seat any of the characters in *Stone Cold.* You will need a volunteer to go into role as the character. The character is then put in the hot-seat.

The rest of the group asks the character questions. You need to find out as much as you can about the character.

COLLISION COURSE – PLOTTING MOVEMENTS

Read the section of novel from 'I trudged along Pentonville
Road' to '…be so unimportant that he'd vanish and no one
would care'. In this section Link meets Ginger. Ginger shows
Link around some of London's landmarks.

- Record in your reading log where Link and Ginger go.

- Record in your reading log where Shelter is. How does he get to Link and Ginger? How do you know this? Does it add excitement to the story?

LINK IN LONDON

- On a photocopy of the map opposite, plot Link's movements in green dots.

SHELTER IN LONDON

- On your photocopy of the map, plot Shelter's movements in red dots.

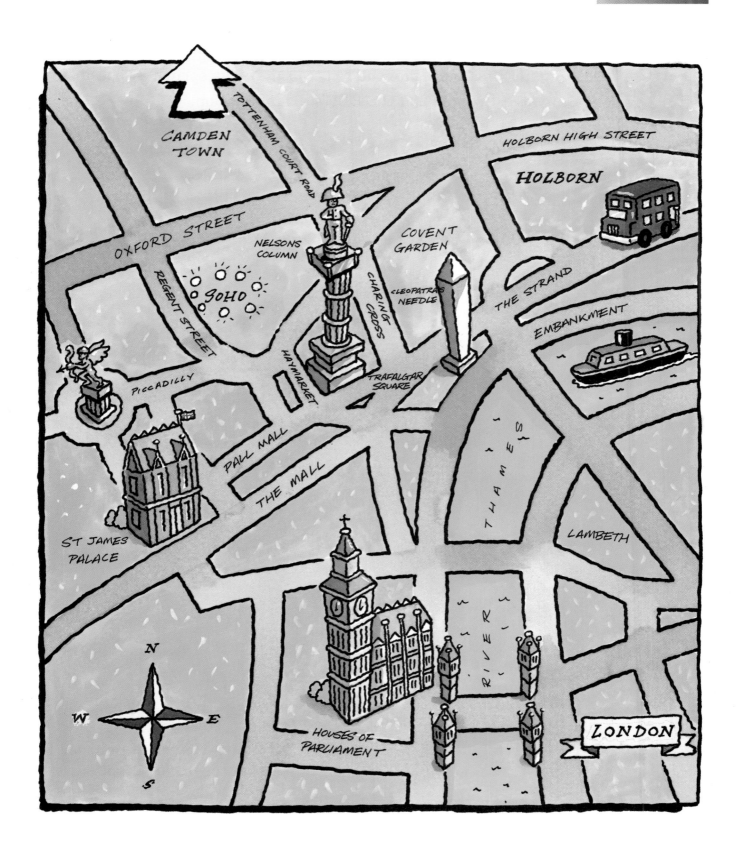

GAIL

Read on to the section which ends 'when something happened to jerk me back into the real world, it was spring.' If possible, watch Episode 2 of the BBC's dramatisation.

Very chatty, lonely?

Very attractive

She's got money

Heads straight for Link – lucky chap!

- Draw a diagram like the one above. Write down all of your thoughts about Gail.
- Stick your diagram into your reading log.

LINK'S DIARY

Dear Diary,

February and cold. Well not any longer!
Today I met the most fantastic-looking
girl. I was in the caff, nursing my
coffee, when in walked Gail...

• Imagine you are Link. Carry on the diary entry above.

• Think about how you feel. Think about the impression that Gail makes on you. Use some details straight from the novel.

HELP

Remember, you are writing to yourself in a diary. Be chatty and informal.

HORROR

Now read this passage from *Stone Cold*. Link finds out what Shelter has been up to – and now his own life is in danger!

There was a short hallway with a door on the right and stairs at the end. The guy pushed open the door with his free hand and stood aside, holding the cat. 'Go on in, young man. I'll be with you in a jiffy.'

The room smelled of polish and was so tidy it looked like nobody used it. Heavy curtains covered the bay window. The only light came from a lamp which stood on a gleaming table. I stood dripping on the guy's immaculate carpet while he carried Sappho through to what I assumed was the kitchen. After a moment he called out, 'You couldn't fetch the dish, could you – the one on the step?'

'Sure.'

'You don't mind?' He chuckled. 'I sometimes think I'd forget my head if it were loose.'

I retrieved the dish with its little heap of mush and carried it through to the kitchen. He had the cat swaddled in a pink towel. 'Thanks.' He smiled. 'Thanks a lot. Just put it down anywhere. I'll get the coat in a minute.'

I went back into the other room, conscious of leaving wet footprints. If I'd entertained lingering suspicions on entering the house they'd now dissolved. The man was obviously a total wally with his cat and his obsessive tidiness. I couldn't help smiling to myself as I surveyed the room. Plumped cushions. Straight pictures. Gleaming surfaces. A place for everything and everything in its place. The occupant of this room was what my grandad used to call a Mary Ellen – the sort of man who wears frilly aprons around the house and may be seen in the garden, pegging out clothes.

I was getting more complacent by the second till I saw my watch on the sideboard.

It was mine, all right. The one I'd handed over to the Scouser about a million years ago. I'd have known it anywhere. There was a tightening sensation in my chest as I stepped over for a closer look, and when the door slammed I cried out.

He'd come in without my hearing. Crossed the room. Was standing now with his broad back against the door, smiling a different smile. He nodded towards the sideboard. 'That was careless of me.' He chuckled, and it was not a wally's chuckle. 'Still, it doesn't matter does it – not now.' He looked at me and hissed, 'Link. Link the Stink. Laughing Boy Two, at last. Whassamatter, Laughing Boy – cat gotcha tongue?' He laughed and called towards the kitchen, 'Hey Sappho – got the kid's tongue, have you?'

I stared at the guy, paralysed with horror. We'd been right, Gail and Nick and me. This was our man. You only had to look in his eyes to know he was mad. He was totally out of his tree and he had me trapped, like Toya and Ginger and –

'Oh, yes.' He'd read my mind. 'He's here, the big Liverpudlian, along with the others, and a promising recruit he's turning out to be, too. Lots of potential. Bags and bags of swank. Would you like to see?'

'No!' It came out as a shriek. I pressed myself against the sideboard. 'I want to go home. Let me go.'

He laughed again, shaking his cropped sandy head. 'Oh no, lad. No going home. Not anymore. You made me wait a long time, but you're in the Army now. The Camden Horizontals. Come and meet your comrades.'

'Let me go!' I knew it was no use, of course I did, but my brain had packed up. I didn't seem to be able to say anything else. He'd gone down on one knee and was lifting a corner of the carpet. I measured the distance to the window. If I could reach it – smash a pane, I thought –

'Here – have a gander.' He'd folded back the carpet and removed three or four short boards from the floor. 'I'll put the big light on so you can see better.' He got up. As he moved towards the switch by the door I made a dash for the window. The light came on. I grabbed for the drapes as he whirled with an oath, coming for me. I wrapped my arms round the curtains and swung on them. There was a creaking, splintering noise as the rail tore loose at one end and swathes of heavy fabric came down on both of us. Sobbing with terror I clawed myself free, slipped my pack and swung it at the window. The pane cracked but failed to shatter, and before I could take a second swing he was on me.

The strength of the insane. I'd come across that phrase, and now found what it meant. I'm not a small guy and he was a lot older but I couldn't break free. I bucked and writhed and lashed out with my feet, but he'd wrapped his arms round me and his grip was like bands of steel. My feet left the floor and he carried me across the room like he'd carried the cat, except he didn't croon or nuzzle, and when we reached the hole in the floor he threw me down and fell on me like a wrestler. I was pinned, lying on my stomach with my head overhanging the hole. A draught rose from the hole, carrying a cloying, sweetish smell. After a few seconds my eyes adjusted to the dimness and I saw them.

There were seven, laid out in a row like sardines. He'd done something to their heads – they were all like his – you couldn't tell if they were girls or boys – but I recognized Ginger by his clothes. His face was – well, I wouldn't have known him from that. I gagged, twisting my head to one side. 'Let me up!' I screamed. 'I'm gonna puke.'

He laughed. 'Puke away, soldier. You're the one'll lie in it, not me.'

With a partner:

- Act out this horrific scene in Shelter's living room
    - use the speech that is used in the novel
    - one person play Link, the other Shelter.
- Think carefully about how each character changes in this scene. Show these changes when you act.

Write about this episode in your log. What makes it so scary?

LINK'S LETTER

Read to the end of the novel.

At the end of the novel how would Link be feeling about Gail and about life in general? He might send her a letter to say how he felt.

> 20th July '98
>
> Dear Gail,
>
> I can't believe what you've done. How could you treat me this way? I thought you cared. I'm so angry now because...
>
>
>
>
>
> Yours,
>
> Link

- Imagine you are Link. Write your letter to Gail. Pass it to a partner to read.

- Consider the points Link would make. Think about how he might sound, e.g. bitter, angry, heart-broken.

- Help each other to improve your letters. You will need to consider the following questions:

  - does this sound like Link?
  - is what he says *clearly* expressed?
  - what else should be put in the letter?
  - has the writer used correct punctuation?

GAIL'S REPLY

Imagine that Gail decides to send her reply to Link on
tape. With a partner:

* Read the letter s/he has written from Link to Gail.

* Imagine you are Gail. Think of the points she would make. Also
consider how she might sound, e.g. sad, guilty, sorry, cold.

* Record your reply to your partner's letter on tape.

SHELTER

It was about 20.00 hours and I'd just begun my nightly patrol.

I marched along the Strand.

Laughing Boy One. That was the code name of the exercise. It was meticulously planned and beautifully executed, and now it's time for debriefing.

The killing, by a soldier, of the enemies of his country is not murder.

My tally of recruits stands at seven.

Tour

They've bags of swank, my lads. Shiny boots and nice short hair.

Check your equipment every time. Run through procedures. Know what's what. Don't fall into any traps.

Khaki

Confront the enemy, Shelter old lad. No retreat. No surrender.

Mission

Volunteers swell the ranks.

The enemy has attacked in strength and has been repulsed.

The Camden Horizontals...

Loners is what you look for in my line of business. Singletons.

...my chief function to kill, waste, do in – whatever you call it...

get fell in, my lucky lads.

DAILY ROUTINE ORDERS 16
(PRISON LIFE)

- Look again at all these extracts from Shelter's Daily Routine Orders. Make a list of all the words and phrases that sound military.

- Imagine that Shelter is now in prison.

- Write some similar Routine Orders. Call your writing 'Shelter's Routine Orders 16 (prison life).'

- Use some of the words and phrases you have listed, and any others you can think of.

EXTENSION TASKS

As an extension to this unit, choose one or two of the following tasks to complete.

1. Gail is a journalist. Write her front page news story. Remember, your headline should make people want to read the story.

2. Would Link return home to Bradford? In small groups role play a family reunion.

3. You have read the novel. You have watched the BBC adaptation. Write a final entry in your reading log to compare the book and film.

4. Did you enjoy Stone Cold? Robert Swindells has written other books. Try reading Brother in the Land or Daz 4 Zoe.

5. Find out more about homelessness. Add the information to your reading log. You could write to:

   Shelter   Centrepoint
   88 Old Street   Bewley House
   London   2 Swallow Place
   EC1V 9HU   London W1R 7AA

6. What do you think about homeless people? Have your views changed now that you have read Stone Cold?